DS 889 T2
                                91-607
Tames, Richard, 1946-

Japan since 1945

THE POST-WAR WORLD

JAPAN
SINCE 1945

RICHARD TAMES

B.T. Batsford Ltd, London

CONTENTS

Typeset by Tek-Art Ltd, Kent
and printed in Great Britain by
The Bath Press,
Bath
for the publishers
B.T. Batsford Ltd
4, Fitzhardinge Street
London W1H 0AH

ISBN 0 7134 5930 1

Acknowledgments
The Author and Publishers would like to
thank the following for permission to
reproduce illustrations: Associated Press
for pages 11, 20, 22 and 54; BBC Hulton
Picture Library for page 15; the Camera
Press for pages 16, 24, 32, 34, 38, 42, 45,
and 52a; Japan Information Centre for
pages 26, 50 and 54; Jetro Photo Service
for page 52b; the Keystone Collection for
pages 9, 12, 22 and 24; Komatsu UK Ltd
for page 56; Magnum Photos Ltd for
pages 30 and 36; Topham Photo Library
for page 6.

Cover illustrations
(*Top*) Expo '70 (courtesy Richard Tames);
(*bottom left*) General MacArthur and
Emperor Hirohito meet in Tokyo,
September 1945 – the first time the
Japanese ruler had ever left his palace to
call on a foreigner; (*bottom centre*)
production line for Datsun cars, 1967;
(*bottom right*) Masako Hosaka, the first
woman executive at the Kanebo
Cosmetics Sales Co.
   The frontispiece shows 19-year-old
student Sakai Yoshinari (born in
Hiroshima on 6 August 1945) lighting the
Olympic flame for the 1964 Tokyo games.

1

1945:THE MEANING OF DEFEAT

John Morris, *Traveller from Tokyo*, 1943.

The Japanese army, as the reader knows, now has complete control of the government. The army in fact *is* the government. Every branch of the national life: education, industry, commerce, even religion, are all now subject to its will.

That army is now committed to a plan of almost unlimited aggression. It must conquer or perish; there is no other alternative. And the people will be ready to support it to the end. The Germans cracked in 1918 . . . . But the psychology of the Japanese people is different, and I believe that they will never give in; they will go on lowering their standard of living, if necessary until the daily ration is barely sufficient to support life, but the people will not crack. It is only by complete physical destruction of their men and their resources that they can be defeated, and until we are in a position to bring this about, any talk of a Japanese collapse is merely a dangerous form of wishful thinking

By 1943, when this warning was written by John Morris – a former teacher of English at Tokyo University – Japan's enemies had learned to take her seriously. Few Westerners knew the Japanese as well as Morris did and those few realized how little their countrymen understood this proud people.

Modernization

In 1868 a revolt overthrew the Tokugawa family which had ruled Japan since 1603, and returned direct power to the young Emperor Meiji. This 'Meiji Restoration' led to a programme of rapid modernization.

In 1853 Japan's policy of voluntary isolation from the world had been forcefully ended when American gunboats demanded that the country be opened up to trade. Japan's response to the threat of foreign domination was an astonishingly successful programme of national modernization along western lines. Eagerly adopting the newest technology, Japan built up a railway system, a powerful army and navy, and vigorous export industries. By 1905 she was strong enough to defeat Russia in a war for control of the Korean peninsula. At the Paris Peace Conference of 1919 Japan was acknowledged as a great power in its own right.

But the Japanese continued to feel that they had not won the true respect of other nations. America and Australia passed laws to keep out Japanese immigrants. British and other Western manufacturers accused their Japanese rivals of using cheap labour and copy-cat methods to dump under-priced goods on the markets of Asia. When world trade collapsed in the 1930s, many Japanese were brought to bankruptcy and near-starvation. Liberal politicians who believed in co-operation with the West were discredited. Increasingly, popular support swung behind military leaders who argued that Japan could only rely on itself and must carve out an empire in East Asia to assure its future security and prosperity.

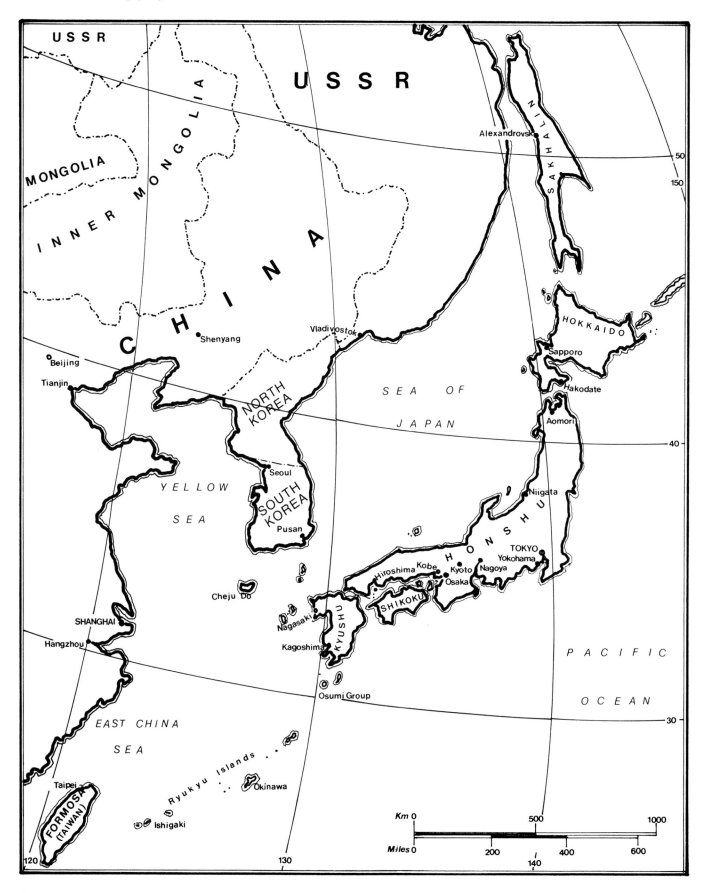

Japan and its neighbours.

Getting There – Yokohama around 1900. Notice the Western-style buildings, English signs, street-lighting and telephone wires. Fifty years before Yokohama had been a tiny fishing village.

Japan's overseas empire was justified as the creation of a 'Greater East Asia Co-Prosperity Sphere', a partnership between industrially developed Japan and the resource-rich mainland.

The average Japanese soldier was 5ft 3ins tall and weighed 117lbs.

Japanese military leaders believed in the power of 'Yamato Damashii' – Japanese Spirit – to overcome the industrial strength of Japan's enemies, trusting that courage and willpower would always defeat mere wealth and numbers.

War

Japan's brutal takeover of Chinese territory during the 1930s provoked protests and economic sanctions from the United States. Accepting conflict as inevitable, Japanese forces seized the initiative, attacked the American naval base at Pearl Harbor and, in swift succession, captured the key British strongholds of Hong Kong and Singapore; then, sweeping onwards, Japanese armies threatened the borders of India itself.

War-time propagandists depicted the Japanese as 'yellow monkeys' – a phrase also used by Hitler, Japan's ally. Victims of their own racism, the Western powers completely underestimated Japan's capacity for war and were bewildered by the ferocity of its onslaught. But, just as Japan seemed everywhere triumphant, the tide began to turn. In June 1942 the Japanese navy suffered its first major defeat in an attack on Midway Island. Having cracked the Japanese radio code, the Americans ambushed the attackers, destroying 300 planes and 21 ships, including four aircraft carriers.

The Allied counter-offensive was two-pronged. General Douglas MacArthur's forces drove through the south-west Pacific, from New Guinea to the Philippines, while those of Admiral Chester Nimitz struck through the islands of the central Pacific, until they could establish secure bases from which Japan itself could be bombed into submission.

The advancing forces met ferocious resistance. It cost the Americans 372 men to take Kwajalein, one of the strategically vital Marshall Islands; the Japanese lost 7870 men in its defence. Of the 32,000 strong garrison on Saipan in the Marianas group only 1000 were left alive when organized resistance ended in July 1944. 10,000 civilians also died. From Saipan US bombers could reach Tokyo. In a three-day raid in March 1945 more than 100,000 civilians were killed or wounded and a million more made homeless.

It was destruction, not death, which brought Japan to its knees. Nothing could replace worn-out or shattered machinery or supply the oil, minerals and food lost at sea to American planes and submarines. Every day their empty bellies told the Japanese people what their leaders dared not say – defeat was inevitable. Nevertheless, the spirit of resistance was undiminished. Between April and June 1945, 100,000 soldiers and civilians died in resisting the American seizure of Okinawa, the last stronghold outside Japan itself.

At the Yalta conference in February 1945 Britain and the USA had received a pledge from the USSR that it would join in the war against Japan 'about 90 days' after Germany's defeat, which came in May. In return the USSR was promised sovereignty over southern Sakhalin and the Kurile islands to the north of Japan. In July, the Japanese government approached the USSR to explore the possibility of its intervention as a neutral power to bring about a negotiated peace. No reply was forthcoming.

Atom bombs and after

At 8.15 a.m. on 6 August 1945 the American bomber Enola Gay dropped a single bomb on the coastal city of Hiroshima, military headquarters of western Japan. It exploded with a force equal to 20,000 tons of TNT, killing or injuring some 200,000 people – some four-fifths of the city's population. Of the 165 doctors in the city, 65 were killed outright, and most of the rest wounded. Of 1780 nurses, 1654 were killed or too badly hurt to tend the injured. At the Red Cross Hospital, the city's best and biggest, one doctor survived uninjured to attend an estimated ten thousand casualties who made their way there for aid. The next day an official radio announcement declared: 'Hiroshima suffered considerable damage as the result of an attack by a few B-29s. It is believed that a new type of bomb was used. The details are being investigated.'

On 8 August Russia's response to Japan's peace feeler was delivered – 'from 9 August the Soviet government will consider itself to be at war with Japan'. Within hours of this declaration a second atomic bomb destroyed the city of Nagasaki.

The Japanese government remained divided until, at a special conference, the Emperor intervened to break the deadlock. On 10 August the Japanese government agreed to accept surrender, except where it involved any 'demand which prejudices the prerogatives of His Majesty as a sovereign ruler'. The US government replied bluntly that 'the authority of the Emperor and the Japanese government to rule the State shall be subject to the Supreme Commander of the Allied Powers.' At a second special conference the Emperor again broke a deadlock by siding with the surrender faction. The

Hiroshima 1945. In the foreground is the shell of a Catholic church.

decision of the Emperor to put his own throne in jeopardy enabled Japan to avoid the possibility of a simultaneous invasion by Soviet and American forces, which would not only have caused many further casualties but also have led to a permanent division of the country – as happened in Germany.

On 15 August the Emperor made his first ever direct broadcast to the Japanese people, calling upon them to join him in his resolve to 'pave the way for a grand peace for all the generations to come by enduring the unendurable and suffering the unsufferable'. After his broadcast more than 500 army and navy officers committed suicide. The reaction of the overwhelming majority of civilians was one of relief – followed by a new fear. What now?

Source A
John Hersey, American journalist, quotes a Japanese civilian's memory of the news of surrender. John Hersey, *Hiroshima*, 1946.

Tenno – literally 'gate', a politely indirect way of referring to the Emperor's palace and hence, indirectly, to the Emperor himself

At the time of the Post-War, the marvellous thing in our history happened. Our Emperor broadcast his own voice through radio directly to us, common people of Japan. August 15th we were told that some news of great importance could be heard and all of us should hear it. So I went to Hiroshima railway station. There was a loudspeaker in the ruins of the station. Many civilians, all of them were in bandages, some being helped by [on the] shoulders of their daughters . . . they listened to the broadcast and when they came to realize the fact that it was the Emperor, they cried with full tears in their eyes. 'What a wonderful blessing it is that Tenno himself calls on us and we can hear his own voice in person. We are thoroughly satisfied in such a great sacrifice.' When they came to know the war was ended – that is, Japan was defeated – they, of course, were deeply disappointed, but followed after their Emperor's commandment in calm spirit, making whole-hearted sacrifice for the everlasting peace of the world – and Japan started her new way.

Source B
Yoshizawa Hisako, a teenage girl, chronicles defeat in her diary. Hashikawa Bunzo *et al.*, *Shimin no Nikki* (*Common People's Diaries*), Shueisha, Tokyo 1965.

August 15
As I listened to the Emperor's voice announcing the surrender, every word acquired a special meaning and His Majesty's voice penetrated my mind. Tears streamed down my cheeks. I kept on telling myself that we must not fight among ourselves and work hard for our common good. Yes, I pledged to myself, I must work . . . .

The volunteer fighting unit was disbanded . . . . Each of us burned the badges . . . I cannot foresee what kind of difficulty will befall me, but all I know is that I must learn to survive, relying on my health and my will to live.

August 16
. . . in place of a 'good morning' or 'good afternoon' people are now greeting each other with the phrase 'What will become of us?' My company announced that until everything becomes clearer, no female employees were to come to work, and urged all of us to go to the countryside, adding that we should leave forwarding addresses. This measure was taken to conform to the step already taken by governmental bureaux. Are they thinking that the occupation army will do something to us girls? There are so many important problems we have to cope with, I cannot understand why governmental officials are so worried about these matters.

We did not have enough power and lost the war.

The Army continued to appeal to the people to resist the enemy to the end. This poses a lot of problems. People can show their true colours better when they are defeated than when they win. I just hope we, as a nation, can show our better side now.

Just because we have been defeated, I do not wish to see us destroying our national characteristics when we are dealing with foreign countries.

August 17
It was rumoured that a number of lower rank military officers were unhappy with the peace and were making secret moves. There were other rumours, and with the quiet evacuation of women and children from the cities, our fear seemed to have intensified. After all we have never experienced a defeat before. Our fear may simply be fear of the unknown . . . .

The defeat of Japan.

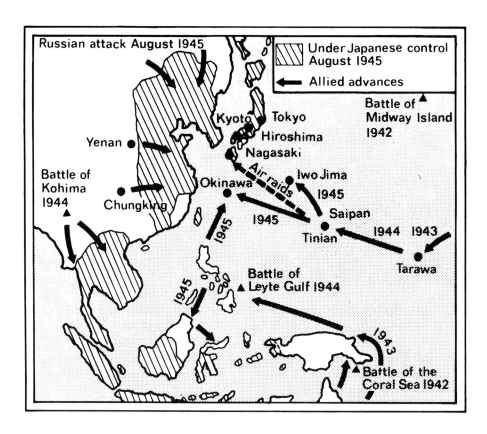

August 21
The fact of a defeat is a very serious matter and it is not easy to accept. However, it can bring some positive effects, if it can impress on our minds all the shortcomings we have had. I hope this will come true one day and toward that end we must all endeavour. Even if we have to suffer hunger and other tribulations we must strive towards a positive goal.

? ?

1 What similarities do you see in the reactions of these two people to the surrender broadcast?

2 What immediate problems would Japanese people face in the wake of defeat?

3 What problems would face the Allied forces coming to occupy Japan?

2 OCCUPATION

MacArthur and the Emperor

From 1945 to 1952 the main aim of Japan's national policy was to regain the right to have one. Japan had lost the war and her empire with it. Her economy was in ruins and her people in a state of shock. For the first time in history she was forced to undergo occupation by the troops of a foreign power – the USA. Both Japan's leaders and people soon saw that the only way back to prosperity and good relations with other countries was by close co-operation with the Americans. Japan would regain its sovereignty – the right to control its own destiny – when the USA decided that it was no longer a danger. So when the Americans landed there was no resistance. The Japanese forces laid down their weapons as obediently as they had once taken them up. And the people set themselves to listen and learn from their conquerors.

In theory the occupation of Japan was an Allied exercise. In practice it was an American one. The Thirteen-nation Far Eastern Commission, sitting in Washington, was too far away for day-to-day control. The Four Power Allied Council for Japan in Tokyo was soon paralyzed by quarrels between the USA and USSR when Soviet requests to occupy half of Hokkaido were turned down. British and Australian forces were present only in token numbers. American troops held almost all of the 2800 foreign bases in the country.

Effective power was concentrated in the hands of one man – General Douglas MacArthur, designated SCAP – Supreme Commander of the Allied Powers. He had very strong ideas about the changes he wanted to bring about. His power was limited in practice by two factors – the abilities and number of his own staff and the willingness of the Japanese to co-operate.

America in the driving seat. GIs take a rickshaw ride round occupied Tokyo. Such sights left no one in any doubt about who had won the war.

The co-operation of one person in particular was to prove essential. While Australian and British politicians pressed the case for the Emperor to be brought to trial as a war criminal, those who knew Japan at first hand, like former US Ambassador Joseph C. Grew, argued that such a course of action would be disastrous. General MacArthur was soon persuaded that the Emperor could make a vital contribution to the realization of the occupation objectives and sent a telegram to General Eisenhower outlining the possible consequences of any attempt to indict him as a war criminal:

No specific and tangible evidence has been uncovered with regard to his exact activities which might connect him in varying degree with the political decisions of the Japanese Empire during the last decade . . . . If he is to be tried great changes must be made in occupational plans . . . . His indictment will unquestionably cause a tremendous convulsion among the Japanese people, the repercussions of which cannot be overestimated. He is a symbol which unites all Japanese. Destroy him and the nation will disintegrate. Practically all Japanese venerate him as the social head of the state and believe, rightly or wrongly, that the Potsdam Agreements were intended to maintain him as Emperor. They will regard allied action [to the contrary as the greatest] betrayal in their history and the hatreds and resentments engendered by this thought will unquestionably last for all measurable time. A vendetta for revenge will thereby be initiated whose cycle may well not be complete for centuries if ever.

The whole of Japan can be expected, in my opinion, to resist the action either by passive or semi-active means. They are disarmed and therefore represent no special menace to trained and equipped troops; but it is not inconceivable that all government agencies will break down . . . and a condition of underground chaos and disorder amounting to guerilla warfare in the mountainous and outlying regions result. I believe all hope of introducing modern democratic methods would disappear and that when military control finally ceased, some form of intensive regimentation, probably along communistic lines, would arise from the mutilated masses.

It is quite possible that a minimum of a million troops would be required which would have to be maintained for an indefinite number of years. In addition a complete civil service might have to be recruited and imported, possibly running into a size of several hundred thousand . . . . Certainly the US should not be called upon to bear unilaterally the terrific burden of manpower, economics and other resultant responsibilities.

The decision as to whether the Emperor should be tried as a war criminal involves a policy determination upon such a high level that I would not feel it appropriate for me to make a recommendation; but if the decision by the heads of states is in the affirmative, I recommend the above measures as imperative.

In fact the Emperor proved eager to co-operate and soon convinced MacArthur that he had 'a more thorough grasp of the democratic concept than almost any Japanese'. On New Year's Day 1946 he issued an Imperial Rescript denying his own status as divine and calling for an immense effort of national reconstruction:

We have to . . . proceed unflinchingly toward elimination of the misguided practices of the past . . . we will construct a new Japan through being thoroughly pacific, the officials and people alike obtaining rich culture and advancing the standard of living . . . . The devastation of the war inflicted upon our cities, the miseries of the destitute, the stagnation of trade, shortage of food and the great and growing number of the unemployed are indeed heart-rending, but if the nation is firmly united in its resolve to face the present ordeal and to see civilization consistently in peace, a bright future will undoubtedly be ours, not only for our country but for the whole of humanity . . . .

Potsdam Agreements: surrender terms offered to Japan by Allied leaders meeting at Potsdam in July 1945.

Forty years on – Emperor Hirohito in the 1980s – a symbol of continuity amid the turmoil of change.

We stand by the people and we wish always to share with them in their moment of joys and sorrows. The ties between us and our people have always stood upon mutual trust and affection. They do not depend upon mere legends and myths. The are not based on the false idea that the Emperor is divine and that the Japanese people are superior to other races and fated to rule the world . . . .

The resolution for the year should be made at the beginning of the year. We expect our people to join us in all exertions looking to accomplishment of this great undertaking in an indomitable spirit.

Source A
John Morris, *Traveller from Tokyo,* Penguin, 1943.

I believe it to be of the utmost importance for the war to be brought home to the people of Japan themselves. They know so little of what is happening in the world today, that only when the war is actually brought to their homeland itself will they realize they are beaten. Nothing less than an occupation of the country will be necessary; not necessarily a very long one, but one long enough to make the fact of our victory and their defeat incontestable. During the period of occupation the demilitarization should be commenced, and it is essential that it should continue until the war-making power of Japan is destroyed . . . . This, then, should be the programme: Defeat, Occupation, Demilitarization, Opportunity. The period of occupation should be made to depend upon the ability of the Japanese to produce a new form of government: a government with liberal ideas that is willing and anxious to co-operate with the Allied Nations. I believe that the nucleus of such a government already exists in Japan. The country has always possessed liberal-minded statesmen . . . . But these men, at the present time, dare not voice their feelings; to do so would be to invite assassination . . . . The chief task of the army of occupation would be to ensure that the new government is afforded protection and help while it is reorganizing the administration of the country . . . .

Any attempt to discredit the Emperor would, in my opinion, be disastrous. What we must do is convince the Japanese people that their Emperor has been led astray by his military advisers. If this could be successfully accomplished it would have the effect of discrediting the army and would thus strengthen the position of the new government. The whole-hearted co-operation of the Emperor would be indispensable.

To sum up, the goal of all our efforts will be to bring into being a peace-loving and contented Japan, an agreeable partner in international politics, a country that will contribute to a single unified world economy. So, if we intend to demilitarize Japan and control her key imports, as it would seem we must, we shall have to find an outlet for her economic energies. We must be careful not to injure the foundations of Japan's economic life; our task is to show her how to build a better structure upon them.

*'These proceedings are now at an end.' General Douglas MacArthur (*far right*) accepts the congratulatory salutes of fellow Allied generals, aboard the USS Missouri. The Japanese delegation, having signed instruments of surrender, stares into an uncertain future.*

Source B
United States Initial Post-Surrender
Policy for Japan

Demilitarization: destruction of military
influence on society.

The ultimate objectives of the United States in regard to Japan . . . are:

(a) To insure that Japan will not again become a menace to the United States or to the peace and security of the world.

(b) To bring about the eventual establishment of a peaceful and responsible government which will respect the rights of other states and will support the objectives of the United States as reflected in the ideals and principles of the Charter of the United Nations.

These objectives will be achieved by the following principal means:

(a) Japan's sovereignty will be limited to the islands of Honshu, Hokkaido, Kyushu, Shikoku and such minor outlying islands as may be determined . . . .

(b) Japan will be completely disarmed and demilitarized. The authority of the militarists and the influence of militarism will be totally eliminated . . . .

(c) The Japanese people shall be encouraged to develop a desire for individual liberties and respect for fundamental human rights, particularly freedoms of religion, assembly, speech and the press. They shall also be encouraged to form democratic and representative organizations.

(d) The Japanese people shall be afforded opportunity to develop for themselves an economy which will permit the peacetime requirements of the population to be met.

? ?

1 Why did the author of Source A lay such stress on the role of the Emperor?

2 In what respects do the authors of the two sources agree?

The 'Showa' Constitution

On 6 March 1946 General MacArthur announced that the government and Emperor of Japan would be presenting a new constitution to the people. While confirming that the Emperor would remain as such, it was misleading in its implication that Japanese leaders would have a hand in framing the rules for the new democracy. In fact it was to be written, in just over a week, by American lawyers serving in their country's armed forces. And it is ironic that this new democratic constitution, whose preamble proclaims that sovereignty springs from the people, was to be presented, like its 'feudalistic' predecessor of 1889, as a gracious gift from the throne.

Mark Gayn, a US Officer deeply involved in drafting the new constitution, tells the inside story:

Whitney (General commanding the section of the Occupation forces dealing with relations with the Japanese government) recited the three points which General MacArthur wanted to see in the new Japanese constitution:

(1) Japan was to renounce war forever, abolish her armed forces and pledge never to revive them;

(2) While sovereignty was to be vested in the people, the Emperor was to be described as a symbol of the state;

(3) The peerage was to be abolished, and the property of the Imperial Household was to revert to the state.

On February 19 General Whitney sprang the constitution on the Japanese: 'Gentlemen, the Supreme Commander has studied the draft prepared by you. He finds it totally unacceptable. I've brought with me a document which has the approval of the Supreme Commander. I'll leave it with you for fifteen minutes, so that you can read it before we discuss it.'

The three Americans then withdrew to the adjoining porch. Through the windows they could see the Japanese huddled over the document. Just about then a US bomber buzzed the house. It was a well-timed incident, even if General Whitney insisted that it had been unscheduled . . . . As General Whitney re-entered the room he said dramatically: 'We've just been basking in the warmth of the atomic sunshine.'

Growing up in a democracy – women cast their vote for the first time in Japanese history, thanks to a constitution written by American servicemen.

The Japanese had no option but to accept, though Gayn himself thought that the enterprise was ultimately doomed:

What is wrong – disastrously wrong – is that this constitution does not come from the Japanese grass roots. It is an alien constitution foisted on the Japanese government and then represented as a native product, when any Japanese high-school student simply by reading it can perceive its foreign origin . . . . And nothing in the constitution is more wrong than General MacArthur's own provision for the renunciation of armed forces. For no one who has read the morning papers or studied Japanese history can doubt that as soon as the occupation ends the Japanese under one pretext or another will re-create their army. That is as inevitable in Japan as earthquakes. By its very nature, the new constitution thus invites circumvention. No constitution in which fraud is inherent can survive.

But in fact it did.

Democracy and Disarmament

Showa: name adopted for the reign of Emperor Hirohito on his accession to the throne in 1926. It means 'Enlightened Peace'.

The Showa constitution became operative on 3 May 1947. It consists of a preamble, stating that 'sovereign power resides with the people', and 103 articles, divided into 11 chapters. The first chapter is devoted not to the rights of the people, but to the position of the Emperor – an acknowledgment of his importance, even when stripped of all power. Article 1 states:

The Emperor shall be the symbol of the state and of the unity of the people.

Article 4 affirms that:

. . . he shall not have powers relating to government.

Article 9 has subsequently been interpreted as permitting the right of national self-defence, as a careful reading of the wording shows it was intended to do.

Chapter II consists solely of Article 9, a unique provision, to be found in no other constitution in the world:

Aspiring sincerely to an international peace based on justice and order, the Japanese people forever renounce war as a sovereign right of the nation and the threat or use of force as a means of settling international disputes.
   In order to accomplish the aim of the preceding paragraph, land, sea and air forces, as well as other war potential, will never be maintained. The right of belligerency of the state will not be recognized.

Chapter III – 'Rights and Duties of the People' – is the longest section, consisting of Articles 10 to 40. The tone, and sometimes the actual wording, echoes closely the constitution of the United States. Article 13, for example, decrees that:

All of the people should be respected as individuals. Their right to life, liberty and the pursuit of happiness shall, to the extent that it does not interfere with the public welfare, be the supreme consideration in legislation and in other governmental affairs.

An affirmation of individual rights may seem unremarkable to a western reader, but it amounted to a wholesale dismissal of the pre-existing legal notion which gave heads of household very real authority over the property, actions and rights of their wives, children and other dependants.

Shinto: 'the way of the gods' is a tradition of rituals, showing reverence for nature, which is unique to Japan.

Article 20 likewise assaulted the old order, which had turned the folk religion of Shinto into a cult of emperor worship. Not only does it proclaim freedom of worship; it also orders that 'no religious organization shall receive any privileges from the State nor exercise any political authority' and bans the State from 'religious education or any other religious activity'.

Other chapters set out the powers and functions of the various organs of government, emphasizing the supremacy of the national Diet (parliament), the independence of the courts and the rights of local government against the power of central government.

Many features of Japanese society seemed hostile to the task of turning the country into a democracy, and in particular the legacy of war-time propaganda which had portrayed the Americans as 'devils' and the general inability of the occupiers to communicate directly with the Japanese in their own language. On the other hand, the Japanese were a highly-educated people whom it was possible to inform through a well-developed press. There were also many political and labour leaders and intellectuals who had clung on to liberal and democratic ideals, despite persecution, and who might provide new leadership for change. And there was the general disillusionment with the militarists who had brought the nation to its state of humiliation and despair. Finally there was the personality of MacArthur himself, a larger than life character, prone to bold gestures, fearless, and convinced of his personal destiny to reshape the history of his defeated enemy. In carrying out this task he had the undoubted advantage of supreme and undisputed authority. There were no Allied zones or partners, as in Germany. And Japan was effectively cut off from the rest of the world because the occupation authorities themselves decided who could leave the country and which foreigners could enter it.

But for MacArthur's objectives to be realized the co-operation of the Japanese was essential, and this assured a certain continuity with the past. There was no realistic option open to the Americans except to work through the existing machinery of the Japanese state which, despite the collapse of the economy, survived more or less intact. Ordinary Japanese people were used to obeying their own officials and policemen and few Americans had any detailed knowledge of Japan. Even fewer were at all fluent in Japanese. So the occupation reforms were, for the most part, put into effect by Japanese personnel. Many of them, such as the enlargement of women's rights, represented a continuation of trends which had begun more than a quarter of a century before or, as in the case of agricultural reform, had long been desired by significant but previously powerless interests.

Democracy was accompanied by demilitarization, which meant far more than mere disarmament. A Study Group convened by the British Royal Institute of International Affairs in 1945 warned that:

If a repetition of the present catastrophe is to be prevented Japanese militarism must be destroyed . . . and an essential preliminary to this destruction will be the relegation of the armed forces to their appropriate influence in the state through constitutional reform. But it is very doubtful if the militarist obsession of the Japanese imagination can be removed by external pressure . . . the most effective antidote will be the liberation of thought and the re-education of the younger generation in an atmosphere of social and economic security.

Disarming Japan's forces was smoothly accomplished and by November 1945 demobilization was virtually complete. Except for those in Russian hands, most overseas troops had been repatriated to Japan. By January 1946 the machinery of war-time repression and censorship had been abolished and an initial 'purge' of militarists begun. As the following table shows, the purges overwhelmingly affected officers and political leaders, rather than officials or businessmen, whose influence on post-war Japan was to be enhanced by the continuity of their involvement in public life.

Victors' justice? Accused Japanese war leaders at the International War Crimes Tribunal. General Tojo Hideki (Prime Minister 1941-4) stands fifth from the left in the middle row.

Category	Number purged
Military	167035
Politicians	34892
Business	1898
Officials	1809
Others	4654

Japan's overall land area is given to be 377,484 sq.k. – but the official statistics include 4996 sq.k. of the Kurile Islands, north of Hokkaido, which are 'currently occupied by the USSR' (International Society for Educational Information, Inc, Understanding Japan, 1987).

For two years an Allied International Military Tribunal for the Far East sat in Tokyo, trying 25 top Japanese officers and officials accused of war crimes against humanity. Seven were hanged, including ex prime minister General Tojo and the rest imprisoned for sentences ranging from seven years to life. Many of these sentences were to be commuted later. Individual Allied countries also held war crimes trials of Japanese. Not surprisingly, these proceedings were considered by many Japanese to be 'victor's justice', with no proper foundation in pre-existing international law.

In the field of education a similar purge cleared out teachers who had been ardent nationalists and opened the ranks of the profession to previously banned left-wingers. Text-books were rewritten to eliminate nationalist propaganda. Compulsory education was extended from six to nine years and made free.

But what chance would infant democracy stand in a country on the edge of starvation? The war had cost Japan 1,855,000 dead and 678,000 wounded or missing. The loss of Taiwan, Sakhalin, Okinawa and various Pacific islands had reduced her national territory by almost a half and the repatriation of their Japanese inhabitants added some 6,000,000 mouths to feed to the already overburdened population. Withdrawal from northern China, Manchuria and Korea cut off valuable supplies of coal, iron, rice, soy beans and salt. Allied air-attacks had cost Japan 80 per cent of her shipping, a third of her industrial machinery and a quarter of her building stock. Industrial production in 1946 was back to what it had been twenty years earlier.

The occupation authorities offered no initial hope of salvation, though the Japanese were more than pleasantly surprised to find that not only did they not propose to live by plunder, they even rushed in emergency relief to avoid mass-starvation. However, a directive from the US government to General MacArthur made it clear that:

You will not assume any responsibility for the economic rehabilitation of Japan or the strengthening of the Japanese economy. You will make it clear to the Japanese people that:
(a) You will assume no obligations to maintain, or have maintained, any particular standard of living in Japan, and
(b) That the standard of living will depend upon the thoroughness with which Japan rids itself of all military ambitions, redirects the use of its human and natural resources wholly and solely for purposes of peaceful living, administers adequate economic and financial controls and co-operates with the occupying forces and the governments they represent.

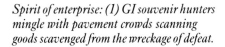

Spirit of enterprise: (1) GI souvenir hunters mingle with pavement crowds scanning goods scavenged from the wreckage of defeat.

The immediate post-war years were dominated by shortages, inflation and rampant petty crime. Only the black market seemed to be doing well. The war had destroyed much but it also had a positive side, spreading useful industrial skills among the Japanese labour force. Service in the army introduced millions of peasants for the first time in their lives to the mysteries of the motor-lorry, the telephone and the radio. And radios, cameras and lorries made for war purposes could one day be redesigned for civilian use. Where factories and transport facilities had been demolished by bombing they could be replaced by the most up-to-date versions available. Throughout history, Japanese villagers had shown their ability to rebuild after fires, earthquakes and other disasters. Now, instead of rebuilding a single village they were going to have to rebuild a whole nation.

Although the Americans initially aimed to break up Japan's heavy industries, which had enabled her to make war, and to dissolve the major industrial combines (Zaibatsu) which had helped to manage the war economy, they gave first priority to land reform.

Small farmers were the largest single category of Japanese workers, accounting for about half the entire labour force. Almost half the nation's land was worked by tenants who paid their rent by turning over much of what they grew to an absentee landlord.

Spirit of enterprise: (2) Growing rice was still back-breaking work but at least the land reform gave the crops to the farmer, instead of the landlord.

The occupation authorities' land reform – which incorporated many suggestions put forward by the Japanese themselves – had two main aims. The first was to diminish the power of landlords, especially absentees, whom they regarded as 'feudal' and therefore hostile to democracy. The second was to create a class of prosperous owner-farmers who would support the new regime because it had given them their land. It was hoped that this would also make them less interested in communism. The land reforms therefore forbade anyone to own more than 2½ acres, unless they cultivated it themselves, in which case the limit was 7½ (in under-populated Hokkaido the limits were higher).

All surplus land was bought by the government at 1939 prices and resold to farmer tenants who bought it with vastly inflated 1947 currency. In practice this might mean acquiring a farm for little more than the price of a few packs of cigarettes – virtual confiscation under cover of law. Some 5,000,000 acres of arable land was redistributed to nearly as many tenant farmers. Rents in general were much reduced and payment in kind virtually disappeared. Only about 10 per cent of the cultivated area was left to be worked by tenants. But, on the negative side, the land reform froze the pattern of farming into small and scattered plots and, while it gave the farmer the incentive to improve what was now truly his own land, it did little to give him the necessary means.

Zaibatsu: industrial combines. They had been vital to Japan's war-effort

In 1946 the 'big four' Zaibatsu – Mitsui, Mitsubishi, Sumitomo and Yasuda – accounted for a third of all Japan's heavy industry and half of its financial strength. The occupation authorities took the view that:

Whether or not individual Zaibatsu were warmongers is relatively unimportant; what matters is that the Zaibatsu system has provided a setting favourable to military aggression.

It was also believed that the Zaibatsu had held down wages, held back the growth of small businesses and prevented the emergence of free trade unions. Their break-up was therefore also desirable on democratic grounds. But it never happened. Other reforms were given priority over the immensely complex task of reorganizing industry and finance. By the time these more urgent tasks had been tackled the attitude of the Americans had begun to change decisively.

As early as March 1947 MacArthur made it clear that Japan's acceptance of reform had been so encouraging that the occupation could be brought to an early end. The spread of Communist power in Eastern Europe after 1945 and the rise of Communist power in China also led to change in attitudes towards Japan. No longer a defeated enemy to be treated with suspicion and disdain, it was now seen as a budding democracy to be fostered as a valued ally. More and more effective power passed into the hands of the Japanese government. SCAP virtually ceased to initiate reforms and confined its role to general overall supervision.

SCAP became a shorthand expression for the occupying Allied Powers.

Industry was encouraged to rebuild. In 1948 the right to strike was limited by law. In 1950, when Communist forces invaded south Korea, a 'red purge' drove 12,000 alleged Communists out of the Japanese union leadership and, at the request of MacArthur, the Japanese established a 75,000 strong National Police Reserve, which was to become the nucleus of today's Self-Defence Forces. Indeed by 1951 Prime Minister Yoshida was telling the Diet that 'large-scale armaments are something that defeated Japan cannot afford to undertake.'

There was nothing inevitable about Japan's transition to democracy and prosperity. Japan had the potential – a tradition of parliamentary government since 1889 – but it also had a recent history of mass-mobilization by military fanatics. Had Japan been occupied by the USSR it might have become a

Communist state. Had it been divided its later history might have been as tragic as that of Korea. That the occupation preserved elements of the Japanese past as well as setting the nation on a new course is a tribute both to the resilience and discipline of the Japanese and to the self-confidence and idealism of the Americans.

Source A

Yoshida Kenichi, journalist and son of Prime Minister Yoshida, argues that Americans deceive themselves about the extent of their influence. From *Japan is a Circle*, Paul Norbury Publications, 1976.

Tin Fords ran in our streets almost as soon as they wre invented in America. American films enthralled us while they were still in their infancy . . . What really happened after the war must have been this. All English words and as many English and American things as [possible] were banned during the war years . . . . So when the Americans landed there were no American shows or cocktails . . . . They came back with the Americans with redoubled fury . . . because we had been so long deprived of hot dogs and cocktails and American shows. But few of the Americans who came knew this. They thought they had succeeded so well in winning us over to their way of life that we had gone suddenly and madly American . . . with that genius for imitation for which we are supposed to be famous. In the wake of these things came democracy . . . If we Japanese can become cocktailshakers in three weeks, we ought to be democrats in four . . . .

The Americans took the line that there was no such thing as democracy until they came and they pointed to the war as evidence. Why should democrats want to fight with America? The struggles we had to evolve a workable representative system or over universal suffrage were just a dead past to them . . . .

. . . like all major wars the war did bring about changes on a vast scale . . . we must look on these changes as changes, and not as examples of Americanization, even when the two seem to coincide superficially . . . . It [the war] has taken away . . . an army constructed on obsolescent principles with an obsolescent mentality to match . . . . It has called the Communists out into the open . . . and now we can fight them without fear of the police coming down on them and turning them into martyrs . . . . The Emperor has once more become the Emperor of the People . . . we do see these changes which would never have been effected except for the war and, what is most important, if we had not lost the war. This is something we really and truly owe the Americans: that they defeated us in such a way as to leave no room for doubt as to who had won. But one cannot call that influence; it was action.

Source B

Thedore Cohen, who as a member of MacArthur's staff was responsible for establishing Japan's free trade unions, argues that the reformers created something greater than they knew. From *Remaking Japan*, Free Press, 1987.

. . . what emerged unexpectedly . . . was the phenomenal development of a mass-production and mass-consumption society. Disarmament and demilitarization did remove the principal obstacles to the development of peaceful industry. That much was planned. But what was not was that democratization, especially economic democratization, notably the liberation of the peasantry and the freedom of labour unions to bargain collectively, created for the first time in Japan's history a domestic mass-consumer market in depth. It was the mainspring of subsequent Japanese economic development and all else that followed. American leaders and their occupation officials did not look ahead far enough to visualize these consequences. They were engrossed in preventing the resurgence of Japanese militarism and building democratic bulwarks against it. Nor did the Japanese see that far ahead at the time. They were happy to have their erstwhile domestic oppressors off their backs and a peaceful 'cultural Japan' in prospect . . . . The Americans got what they thought they wanted and so did the Japanese. What they got in addition was an 'economic miracle'.

? ?

1 Why does the author of Source A think the Americans misunderstood what was going on around them?

2 What did the author of Source B mean by 'economic democratization'?

3 In what way do the authors of the two sources agree about the way history happens?

3 JAPAN EMERGES 1953~64

In America's Shadow

On 8 September 1951 Prime Minister Yoshida Shigeru signed a peace treaty with the United States at a ceremony in the Opera House at San Francisco. Britain, France and a number of America's other allies were co-signatories. The USSR and its allies were not. Yoshida was staking his political life on this 'majority peace', despite opposition within Japan from idealists who insisted that only an 'overall peace' could guarantee Japan's security. Yoshida believed that in the prevailing conditions of international politics this was a practical impossibility. The 'Cold War' between the USA and the USSR forced every country to choose to be on one side or the other. Japan had already been tied to the United States by six years of occupation. Better to accept the alliance with enthusiasm, Yoshida thought, than try to wriggle out of it for no certain alternative. 'Unarmed neutrality' might appeal to university pacifists. To an experienced diplomat like Yoshida it looked like an open invitation to be bullied by the well-armed Communist powers. Five hours after signing the peace treaty Yoshida signed a Treaty of Mutual Co-Operation and Security between Japan and the United States. This gave the US the right to continue to maintain garrisons on Japanese soil and to intervene in the event of internal disturbances in Japan. The US was in return bound to defend Japan but Japan had no reciprocal obligation to assist it. No definite date was set for the termination of the treaty.

Yoshida's decision carried a high political price. Japanese public opinion remained divided about the wisdom of his choice; this was inevitable perhaps in any democracy but difficult to get used to in a country which had set such high store by national unity for so many years. More serious perhaps was the perpetuation of bad relations with the USSR, which refused to contemplate evacuation of the Kurile islands (claimed by Japan as national territory) and used its veto on the Security Council to block Japan's entry to the United Nations. Another unwelcome consequence of the American alliance was the necessity to recognize Chiang Kai-Shek's Nationalist regime in Taiwan as the legitimate government of China and not the Communist People's Republic which actually controlled the country. Loyalty to the United States meant loyalty to its protégés as well.

The San Francisco Peace Treaty took effect on 28 April 1952 and SCAP was accordingly disbanded on that date. Three days later left-wing demonstrators organized an anti-American riot outside the Imperial Palace. One student was killed in the disorder and over 1000 people arrested. It was a crude reminder that many Japanese deeply resented the continuing presence of 260,000 American troops in their country. Yoshida remained

A chapter closes, a chapter opens – Japanese Prime Minister Yoshida Shigeru signs a Treaty of Mutual Co-operation and Security with the USA in San Francisco, 1951.

The 'Northern Territories' issue remains unresolved at the time of writing (1989).

unrepentant about the American alliance, despite a dramatic fall in his personal popularity and stinging parliamentary criticism of his self-assured style as 'one man rule'. In November 1954 he finally resigned as Prime Minister, to be succeeded by Hatoyama Ichiro – a tough professional politician who was known to be distinctly less pro-American than his predecessor.

Hatoyama threw his main effort into re-establishing diplomatic relations with the USSR, a goal finally achieved in October 1956. The problematic issue of the Kurile islands was, however, side-stepped rather than solved; Russian occupation continued and while *de facto* relations operated, no definitive peace treaty was signed. Two months later Japan was at last admitted to the United Nations.

When Kishi Nobusuke took over as Prime Minister he felt obliged to follow his predecessors by scoring a similar triumph in foreign policy and set his sights on a revision of the security treaty with the United States. His proposals included:

(a) limiting the period of a renewed treaty to ten years
(b) requiring the United States to consult the Japanese government before changing the deployment of American troops
(c) involving Japanese forces in joint defence activities
(d) ending the American right to intervene in Japanese domestic politics
(e) forbidding nuclear weapons to be located on Japanese soil without Japanese consent
(f) ending Japanese payments for the presence of US troops.

Although these terms considerably enhanced Japan's status in the alliance, which would become much more of an equal partnership, there soon arose a massive wave of popular opposition to the revised treaty and the relationship it represented. Many Japanese, especially on the left wing, objected to the continuing estrangement from Communist China and Russia. Others feared that a Japan more active in its own defence might become a fully rearmed Japan. The Socialist Party, as the largest opposition group, took the lead in blocking discussion of the treaty in the Diet. Kishi was undeterred and his ruling Liberal Democratic Party had a clear majority. When the Socialists rejected his proposal for an extension of the parliamentary session to allow for further consideration of the treaty, he used his majority to force a vote approving the extension nonetheless.

This perfectly legal action was thought by many – even inside Kishi's own party – to be very 'un-Japanese'. The proper course of action for a truly national leader would be patiently to seek consensus through compromise, particularly when dealing with basic issues of security. Enraged Socialist deputies therefore boycotted parliamentary sessions and daily street demonstrations, involving hundreds of thousands of protesters, were organized by trade unions and student groups. There were several ugly anti-American incidents and, in the circumstances, President Eisenhower was obliged to cancel a long-scheduled goodwill visit. Kishi nevertheless pressed forward with the ratification of the treaty, claiming that he was listening to the 'mute voice' of the majority rather than the slogan-chanting crowds on the streets. He resigned almost immediately after the treaty was secured and the agitation died away almost as quickly as it had arisen.

The resolution of other outstanding issues between the United States and Japan caused no great concern. In 1960 the United States paroled the last one hundred war criminals, held in prison in Tokyo. In 1962 agreement was finally reached over Japan's contribution to the costs of the occupation: $490,000,000, a quarter of the estimated total, was to be repaid over 15 years. Most of the money was in practice to go to developing countries with which both the US and Japan wished to strengthen relations, a fitting symbol of the way in which a defensive alliance was evolving into a positive force for peace.

Ratification: confirmation through formal channels.

Source A

Paul F. Langer, an American expert on international relations and former member of the Occupation forces, analyses conflicting Japanese attitudes towards the United States (1959).

Popular feeling tends to be strongly influenced by fear of involvement in another war, the nightmarish vision of the Japanese islands as an atomic battlefield . . . Japanese attitudes towards the American alliance range from absolute opposition to a reluctant acknowledgment that the present arrangements are necessary for some time to come . . . . But even the Japanese supporters of military reliance on the US are inclined to doubt the danger of Communist aggression . . . . This feeling, together with a certain lack of confidence in the ability of the United States to protect Japan without destroying it at the same time through involvement in nuclear warfare, and a growing demand for a more independent Japanese foreign policy, is now complicating the problem of the role of the US in the defence of Japan.

**Seven years after foreign occupation Japan's map is still dotted with American military bases. Until these are gone the Japanese people will not fully enjoy their independence nor regain the esteem of the rest of Asia . . . . In a country like Japan every acre diverted from cultivation is a grave loss . . . when, as in . . . Okinawa, more than 20 per cent of the farm land is taken up by military installations, the problem reaches serious proportions . . . .
Japanese resentment explodes intermittently in anti-American campaigns skilfully fanned by the political left. Minor incidents often snowball into huge demonstrations . . . . Moreover the fact that US atomic tests have reduced Japan's Pacific fishing grounds and contaminated Japanese catches has provided the strongly emotional anti-nuclear movement in Japan with an economic basis.**

Source B

Jun Eto, a Tokyo professor, puzzles over the confused events surrounding the renegotiation of the Security Treaty in 1960. From *A Nation Reborn*, International Society for Educational Information, 1974.

The motive that prompted legions of Japanese to join the surging waves of street demonstration around the Diet Building was a complex mixture of three strands of sentiments – (1) antipathy against Kishi, the man, and his seemingly authoritarian political style, (2) opposition to the proposed revision of the Security Treaty and (3) anti-American nationalism. Also complex was the composition of the masses of demonstrators, who numbered no less than 300,000 a day at the peak of the public frenzy.

Outrage on both sides of the political spectrum. Right-wing student Yamaguchi Otaya, aged 17, stabs Asanuma Inejiro, leader of the Japan Socialist Party, in October 1960. Asanuma died hours afterwards. Ex-Prime Minister Kishi was stabbed by another right-wing fanatic during the same year.

A clash of opinion: 6000 police frustrate the efforts of 7000 students to storm the National Diet building during debates on the revision of the US Security Treaty. Newsmen take a detached view from the roofs of police armoured cars.

One important factor that helped the mass agitation to explode the way it did and eventually topple the government was the extraordinary development of the mass media – a phenomenon that was almost unthinkable before the 1960s. The press, TV and weekly magazines joined together to feed the public with graphic accounts of the riotous demonstrations, projecting an image out of all proportion to the real substance of the phenomenon. Indeed, the treaty upheaval brought home to all those concerned the unprecedented difficulty of governing [the] modern mass society into which Japan was developing....

Kishi's tragic plight stemmed from his failure to win the mass media to his side and utilize them as a medium of putting his ideas across to the nation despite his keen recognition of television's great role in modern society.

At the extraordinary convention of the Liberal-Democratic Party on July 18 1960 Kishi announced his intention to give up ... the premiership .... At a reception held in honour of (his successor) Kishi was stabbed by a right-wing fanatic. The episode reflected the political confusion that prevailed in Japan at that time.

? ?

1 Apart from the reasons given in Source A, what other objections do you think Japanese might have had at this time to increased spending on defence?

2 Source B stresses the wide range of opposition to the 1960 treaty. Why do you think Kishi was attacked by a *right-wing* fanatic?

Road to Recovery

The outbreak of the Korean war in 1950 brought unexpected economic benefits to Japan in the form of 'special procurements' by US military forces needing supplies and provisions and from spending by US servicemen on leave for 'rest and recreation'. By 1952 the income from special procurements was sufficient to pay for half of all Japan's imports. The United States therefore decided that the time had come to end the grants it had been giving Japan to help rebuild its economy. By 1952 this aid had amounted to $2016 million. Even after the Korean war ended in 1953, however, spending by US troops stationed in Japan or visiting from Korea or other Asian countries amounted to some $500 million a year.

By 1954 Japanese average incomes were back where they had been in the mid 1930s, before the pressures of war had distorted and ultimately shattered the economy.

In 1955 the Cabinet of Prime Minister Hatoyama mapped out Japan's future industrial strategy in a 'Five Year Plan for Economic Self-Support'. Its primary aim was the 'achievement of a viable economy without reliance on special procurements' and it hoped that Japan would achieve an annual average growth rate of 5 per cent in its Gross National Product throughout the period 1955-60. In fact the economy grew nearly twice as fast as had been envisaged. Many targets for the modernization of export industries were achieved in two years rather than the envisioned five, and by 1957 living standards were already 27 per cent higher than they had been in 1954. By 1958 a government survey could proclaim that the recovery from war-time destruction was now complete; but it warned that in future economic growth would be much less rapid.

Export-led growth. A British ship loads up with goods 'Made in Japan'.

Events continued to confound such cautious prophecies. Between 1956 and 1959 a whole new industry established itself as television ownership rose from 165,000 sets to 3,290,000 – a twenty-fold increase in just three years.

When Ikeda Hayato, a public finance expert, took over as Prime Minister in 1960 he boldly unveiled a 'National Income Doubling Plan', which he promised would make the nation twice as well off in just ten years. Western observers scoffed at such foolishness. As it turned out the target was to be achieved in just seven years.

The detail of the Ikeda Plan was largely drawn up under the direction of Okita Saburo, a future Foreign Minister. It recognized five major priorities for development:

(1) Improvement of Japan's 'infrastructure' – i.e. roads, harbours, water and sewage systems. Together with the construction of low-rent public housing this should stimulate growth in the steel and materials industries, as well as removing bottlenecks to growth.

Host to the World. Nineteen-year-old student Sakai Yoshinari, born in Hiroshima on the day the A-bomb was dropped, lights the Olympic flame.

Bullet train – capable of 200 kilometres per hour.

(2) Encouragement of heavy industry, especially in chemicals and machinery. These industries were recognized as important in their own right but also as critical to the growth of a whole range of other industries.

(3) Promotion of exports and expansion of links with developing countries. Motor vehicles were seen as a leading future industry and the importance of developing countries as markets with great growth potential was recognized.

(4) Enhancement of Japan's 'human resources' through setting targets for increases in the number of university graduates in science and technololgy and in spending on research and vocational training.

(5) Narrowing the gaps between modernized and traditional industries and between rapidly prospering and more backward regions.

Ikeda's Plan did not mean that Japan was becoming a Communist-style 'command economy' in which the government controlled economic life in detail. If anything, the Japanese government favoured a tougher, more competitive free-market style of capitalism than many Western countries did at that time. But it did also recognize that government could play a vital part in creating conditions in which industry could thrive – by public investment in communications, by maintaining a stable currency, by granting 'tax holidays' to encourage investment in equipment and training, by imposing tariffs on foreign imports until Japanese manufacturers were efficient enough to meet competition without such protection, by keeping taxes on business low and by setting out a broad picture of how the economy as a whole might reasonably be expected to develop in the foreseeable future.

Japanese governments' willingness to arrange national policy around the principles of 'economy first, production first, exports first' was to play havoc with the environment but this was not to become obvious until the end of a 'miraculous' decade of unprecedented economic expansion. In the meantime, international recognition of Japan's astonishing success came in the form of admission to the Organization for Economic Co-Operation and Development, the 'club' of rich nations, in 1964. And in the same year Japan basked in the attention of the world's news media as she hosted the Olympic Games with flair and efficiency, shuttling awe-struck visitors between Tokyo and Kyoto on the 130mph 'bullet train', specially inaugurated for the occasion. Truly the Asian phoenix had risen from the ashes of defeat.

Source A
Fukutake Tadashi, a Japanese sociologist, reflects on the hesitant pace of change in the countryside. From 'Rural Society' in the *International Social Service Journal* Vol. XIII, UNESCO, 1961.

As of 1955 the number of agricultural households was 6,040,000 or 34 per cent of the total number of households. Agricultural families, however, comprised some 36,470,000 persons, representing 41 per cent of the total population, indicating that the proportion of peasants to the total, despite the steady decline in the past, is not yet small . . . . In 'pre-reform' days peasants had no wish to improve the productivity of land because it was very likely that landowners would take arable land of high productivity away from them and because increased crops meant an increase in the rental rate. Today, on the contrary, increased crops automatically mean an increase in farmers' incomes. Accordingly, they have begun to study new farming techniques, as indicated by the increased sales of technical books and magazines. The government, for its part, has been trying to raise farmers' technical standards by sending a number of 'extension workers' to rural communities . . . .

The rapid increase in production and the development of farm techniques may both be partly ascribed to the increased uses of mechanical power. Only 90,000 electric motors were used by farmers in 1939; today, more than 2.5 million mechanical power sources . . . are employed. . . .

Farmers' living standards have also been improved . . . . Their consumption level, if taken as 100 for the 1934-6 period, climbed to 109.4 in 1951 . . . and soared to 133.8 in 1956 . . . . The living standard of farmers has risen but it is still much lower than that of urban residents. Japanese rural society is still poor . . . . The per capita income of farmers was only 83 per cent of that of urban industrial workers as of 1952. It declined to 67 per cent in 1956 and this downward trend continues . . . .

Farmers' attitudes towards community life have changed greatly . . . . Today, they are prone to regard themselves as 'agricultural entrepreneurs' or even as 'businessmen' . . . . Contacts with urban residents have become more frequent because more members of rural families are working in urban industries. This has accelerated the swift urbanization of rural society . . . . [But] The growth of democratic rural society is not yet complete . . . . Post-war rural reform programmes . . . have failed to remove completely the deep-rooted impediments to the development of democracy in rural society. This may be ascribed to the fact that most Japanese peasants depend on extremely small farms and are hence unable to gain full economic independence . . . people cannot develop democracy in their society while obliged to fight against poverty. The only means of coping with the difficulties in Japanese rural society is to reduce the chronic population pressure and make modern industries absorb those peasants who are engaged in outside jobs . . . it is essential to provide more opportunities for economic independence of agrarian families . . . .

? ?

1 Why does the author believe that economic improvement is necessary for the emergence of a more active democracy in the country areas?

2 In what ways does change in the countryside appear to depend upon change in urban areas?

4 THE YEARS OF THE MIRACLE
1965-72

Supergrowth

From the autumn of 1965 to the summer of 1970 Japan passed through a period of uninterrupted economic boom, with the annual growth rate *averaging* a staggering 11 per cent, thanks largely to the even more rapid rate of investment in plant and equipment, which averaged more than 20 per cent. In 1967 Japan was proud to proclaim that it had become the second largest economy in the non-communist world, surpassed only by the USA.

In the course of these years Japan's international trade position was also radically changed. Whereas world trade as a whole was expanding at around 8 per cent in the mid 1960s, Japan's exports were growing twice as fast, fuelled both by the competitiveness of her newly-equipped industries and the extraordinary demand for 'special procurements' which arose from the stepping up of America's role in the Vietnam war. As a result, Japan's balance of trade moved into surplus for the first time in 1968 – and stayed there. Her foreign exchange reserves rose from $3.5 billion in 1969 to $5.5 billion in 1970 – and a whopping $15.2 billion by 1971.

A Nissan production line 1967. Japanese cars won a reputation for reliability and their makers won fame for their productivity and model industrial relations.

This era of rapid growth saw important changes in both the pattern of Japan's economic activity and the structure and organization of its industry. Products of the heavy metals, engineering and chemical industries became increasingly important as exports, while traditional light industry products – such as textiles and toys – shrank into relative insignificance. Imports came to consist almost entirely of oil, minerals, wood pulp and other raw materials to keep industry expanding still further.

For the first time Japan was now wealthy enough to begin investing overseas, developing mines and plantations to assure future raw material supplies and even relocating manufacturing in developing countries to take advantage of lower labour costs.

In Japan itself a labour shortage began to appear and wage rates began to rise by 15 per cent per year, rather than the 5 per cent or so which had previously been the norm. In response to the lure of higher wages the inflow of workers from the countryside to the cities became a flood and the number of purely agricultural households fell as even country people found part-time employment in workshops and offices.

The most rapidly growing sector of the economy was what is broadly called 'machinery', as the following output figures show:

	Transistor radios	*Colour TVs*	*Motor cars*
1965	454,000,000	98,000	696,000
1970	1,813,000,000	6,399,000	3,178,000

Although many of these consumer goods went for export, the main focus of their manufacturers was the massive market in Japan. Japan's population passed the 100 million mark in 1967 and the simplicity of traditional Japanese life-styles was giving way rapidly to a taste for gadgets and novelties, as the memory of war and its poverty receded.

When a Japanese Emperor is crowned he receives 'three treasures' – a mirror, sword and jewel – as symbols of his authority. By the 1950s, Japanese consumers had begun to covet their own 'three treasures' – a television, refrigerator and washing machine. By the early 1960s these had become the '3 Cs' – car, 'cooler' (air conditioning) and colour (TV). By the late 1960s the ambitious aspired to the '3 Vs' – a villa by the sea or in the mountains, regular vacations and a visit to a foreign country.

In a society increasingly driven by material ambitions the attainment of secure, well-paid employment was seen to be crucial. In Japan, recruitment to this sort of job increasingly came to require high levels of educational attainment – at least staying on through senior high school and preferably going on to college or university. This put a real burden on family finances and strengthened the trend to smaller families. It also increased the pressures on pupils to cram as hard as possible. When Japanese students seized control of the elite Tokyo university during the world-wide student disturbances of 1968, at least some commentators were prepared to say that they had a legitimate grievance to protest about.

On the other hand, Japan appeared to many Western visitors to be refreshingly free from some of the ills which plagued other industrial societies. There was no drug problem. Despite urban overcrowding and poor standards of housing, the streets were safe by night and day. Indeed, recorded crime rates were actually falling. Industrial relations were already a legend for harmony around the world, with Japanese workers famous for their hard work and loyalty. Such strikes as there were seemed to be almost a ritual

Mount Fuji broods over the first public showing of the world's largest super-tanker under construction. Japan's industrial achievements became a major source of national pride.

accompaniment to the beginning of the new financial year in April. And this 'spring struggle' was more likely to be over in a matter of hours rather than days – let alone weeks. Western observers could therefore easily persuade themselves that in their social behaviour as much as in their economy, the Japanese had achieved something of a miracle.

Source A

A Japanese government report looks at changes in the nation's health. From *The Japanese and Their Society*, Part II of the Report on National Life, 1972, prepared by the Japanese Government Economic Planning Agency.

According to the Preliminary Life-Span Table of 1971, the average life-span is 70.17 for males and 75.58 for females. This has made Japan join the group of longest-living nations in the world . . . . We also find Japan in the group with the lowest infant mortality, following Holland and equal to Sweden . . . .

The average Japanese seems to have a great concern for health; the survey of awareness on health reveals that the Japanese consider health the most important factor in daily life, and this is particularly true for about 70 per cent of those aged 65 and above. Why do they attach such importance to their health? . . . The largest group of those surveyed points out that health is the basis for everything in human life. But this type of abstract answer appears less frequently as people grow older. Instead of that, realistic reasons are mentioned more often in the aged groups. Fewer people gave such reasons as dislike of physical pain and inability to do things they want to do . . . . These two reasons appear less frequently than such reasons as decline in income and a rise in spending and embarrassing their family . . . . These observations could lead to the conclusion that Japanese awareness of health is centred on consideration for others – especially for their family – rather than on themselves . . . .

. . . sleeping hours and diet are the main concerns of people attempting to maintain health. Only 12 per cent of the people are paying attention to sports and exercises for promoting their positive health. Moreover, as people grow older, sport and exercise activities are reduced and they rely more on tonics . . . . For many of today's people . . . their work is so intensive that accumulation of stress can not easily be avoided by everyday sleep. It seems particularly true in present day Japan, where there is not yet any system of vacation in terms of weeks or months; moreover people do not take more than half of their paid holidays, which are substantially less than those in Western countries . . . .

. . . people are not willing to take sick leave except when they are seriously ill. According to the survey on medical insurance conducted by the Prime Minister's Office in 1967, there was a wide gap between the length of time in which a patient was receiving medical treatment and the length of time in which he was away from work. Forty per cent of those surveyed did not take sick leave while receiving medical care . . . .

Generally speaking improvements in nutrition exert a good effect on people's physiques and physical strength. This has been remarkably demonstrated among youths in Post-War Japan. Their height and weight has increased sharply. We can also see considerable progress in physical strength and ability . . . Keeping exercise balanced with the intake of nutrition has become an important problem for adults, too . . . people are less apt to harm their health from heavy work than before, but they now have fewer occasions for getting exercise through their work.

Exercises to promote positive health will be effective only when people do them continuously . . . (and) utilizing commercial facilities is too expensive to do in routine life for the general public. The importance of accessibility to public facilities in local communities therefore should be stressed. At present such accessibility is quite limited in Japan, especially in big cities where most space is used for economic purposes . . . .

??

1 How does the source reveal the impact of rising affluence on the pattern of health and well-being?

2 How do you think the problem for adults of balancing diet and exercise was affected by changes in their working lives?

Changes in medical facilities 1960-70	
	Per cent change 1960-70
Hospital	+ 30
Clinics	+ 12
Beds per 100,000 people	+ 40
Doctors	+ 14
Nurses	+ 73
Dentists	+ 11
Pharmacists	+ 13

Medical expenditure rose by 380 per cent over the same period.

Pollution

During the 1950s the race to reconstruct was so enthusiastically pursued that few seemed to realize that 'progress' involves a price. Around 1960 a number of dramatic developments began to catch the headlines. Suddenly 'pollution' was news and the Japanese word for it – 'kogai' – became part of everyday speech.

In Gunma prefecture cadmium poisoning of rice produced a brittle bone condition among local people, resulting in painful splintering and fractures. This became known as Itai-Itai disease ('It hurts! It hurts!'). In the city of Minamata in Kyushu mercury poisoning gave rise to 'Minamata disease', which killed 60 people and maimed hundreds more. At Yokkaiichi on Ise Bay near Nagoya a new and massive petrochemical complex led to so-called 'Yokkaiichi asthma' among local residents.

The Japanese rapidly became aware that booming industrial growth didn't just mean new jobs, higher wages and more goods in their homes. It could also mean foul air, soil and water, an ugly landscape, damage to property through vibration and subsidence and endless aggravating noise. 'Citizens' groups' began to organize. In 1964 the residents of Mishima City mounted a campaign to block plans for a new industrial complex at nearby Numazu. Previously localities had competed with one another to lure companies into their areas in the interest of bringing in new jobs; now they actually opposed development. In the same year, and far more spectacularly, students began to back local farmers in their struggle against the building of a new international airport at Narita – on the outskirts of Tokyo – thus launching a campaign of unprecedented violence which would stretch on for years.

In 1965 inhabitants of Niigata prefecture began to suffer from a similar sort of disease to the one which had afflicted the people of Minamata. The culprit was a local chemical company, which denied any liability. In June 1967 the victims of Niigata went to court and brought the first ever major civil suit for damages against a polluter. The people of Minamata followed their example. In both cases the courts eventually found in favour of the victims, though the damages were small and the verdict took years to reach.

In local and municipal elections, left-wing candidates began to realize that they could win votes by campaigning against the big business interests which

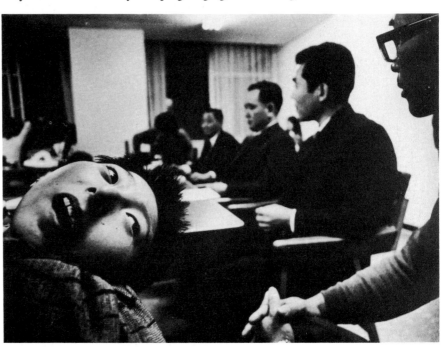

A victim of Minamata disease lies a helpless witness at one of the innumerable meetings held to determine responsibility for the disaster and compensation for the suffering it inflicted.

the public held to be largely responsible for pollution. Once elected as mayors or governors of prefectures they could pass strict laws, requiring factories to control their output of smoke, gases and toxic wastes and restricting the extension of existing industrial sites.

Meanwhile the citizens' groups continued to grow in strength and numbers. By 1971 the Pollution Problems Research Association could list over 450 anti-pollution groups, more than one hundred of them in Tokyo alone. Backed by detailed scientific research and using both the power of publicity and the authority of the courts, these organizations sought to curb every kind of environmental nuisance, from noisy lorries to proposals for tall buildings, which might deprive others of their 'right to light'.

The Japanese government responded to pressure and began to promote counter-measures to bring pollution under control. In 1964 an Environmental Pollution Section was established within the Ministry of Health. In 1965 a Public Nuisance Prevention Corporation was set up. In 1966 a strict new law was passed to regulate the emission of exhaust gases by new cars. In 1967 a Basic Environmental Pollution Prevention Law went into effect and in 1971 a full-blown Environment Agency was set up, headed by a minister with cabinet rank. In 1972 the Agency's Director publicly confessed at a United Nations Conference on the Human Environment that Japan had been wrong to pursue a policy of economic growth regardless of the consequences. The Japanese were now finding out the hard way what some of the consequences were. As a confession by a government leader it was perhaps long overdue, but it did mark a new awareness and a new beginning in official thinking.

Source A

Prime Minister Tanaka offers his vision of Japan's future. From Tanaka Kakuei *Nippon Retto Kaizoron*, (*A Plan to Remodel the Japanese Archipelago*), Tokyo, Nikkon Kogyo Shimbun Sha, 1972.

Man of the people – Tanaka Kakuei campaigning for votes. Note the white gloves traditionally worn by glad-handing politicians.

. . . during the past several years, both domestic and overseas conditions affecting the Japanese economy have suddenly changed. First, private investment in plant and equipment which has been sustaining the favourable cycle (of growth) is showing signs of slowing down. Second, it is no longer possible to expect that the expansion in our exports can be maintained at the same pace as before . . . foreign countries are alarmed by the excessive growth in our exports, and one after another, they are taking measures to curtail them . . . Third . . . problems of overpopulation in large cities and pollution of the environment have intensified . . . . Fourth, there is a trend toward labour shortage, especially shortage of young workers . . . if we cannot expect much from growth in private investment . . . or in exports, we can still look to other areas for factors which can sustain our economy's growth. The first is to expand our social overhead capital investment . . . such as parks, athletic fields, sewage systems, treatment plants, highways and harbours. The people are strongly demanding that we build, equip and expand these facilities. The second is to expand consumption by individuals . . . .

Taking the 1970 GNP of 73 trillion yen as the base and assuming that our national economy will continue to grow at a rate of 10% per year, our GNP in 1985 will reach 304 trillion yen or about $1 trillion . . . . The question we have to face is how to handle this economy, which will be as large as the American economy is today, in the four islands of Japan which are one-thirtieth the size of the United States . . . in addition to the perspective of economic growth, we must select our industrial structure with a view to making our country a better place to live and work in. In other words, heavy industries and chemical industries are not going to be our leading industries. We must select industries with these new yardsticks: 'Will the prospective industry pollute and destroy our natural environment? Will the people be able to engage in their tasks with pride and joy?'

We plan to develop the following types of industries: research and development intensive industries (including electronic, computer, aircraft, electric car, industrial robot and oceanic development industries); fashion industries (high fashion, furniture and household equipment industries); and advanced assembly industries (communications equipment, business

Man of letters (1): Kawabata Yasunari becomes the first Japanese to win the Nobel Prize for Literature in 1968.

Man of Letters (2): Mishima Yukio, post-war Japan's most prolific and versatile writer, shortly before he committed suicide by seppuku (ritual disembowelment) in 1970, after a failed coup in the name of the Emperor.

Archipelago: group of islands.

machine, anti-pollution equipment and teaching machine industries . . . .) It is possible to remodel the Japanese archipelago into a richer, less polluted and livable place. To do so we must decisively change the current trend which forces an extreme concentration of industries, population and cultural activities in our major cities.

? ?

1 What difficulties and dangers can you see in this programme?
2 How far has Tanaka's vision been realized?

Gently Does It

1964 was the first year in which ordinary Japanese citizens could leave the country without going through a long and complex procedure to get a special visa. This reflected both the emerging strength of Japan's economy and a more relaxed attitude towards contacts with the rest of the world. But foreign policy itself was still strictly conducted within a framework of fundamental reliance on the United States. To a considerable extent Japan's foreign policy was independent only in the technical sense that it wasn't actually dictated from Washington.

In 1965, after a 20 year gap, Japan succeeded in re-establishing normal diplomatic relations with South Korea, its nearest neighbour. Harshly ruled as a Japanese colony from 1910 to 1945, Korea was now emerging as a new industrial power Japan could not afford to ignore. The renewal of official contacts in 1965 scarcely healed old wounds but it did allow a prickly

Great Leap Forward: an abortive attempt at forced industrialization in the late 1950s.

Cultural Revolution: a wide-ranging campaign, inspired by Communist Party Chairman Mao Zedong, to re-invigorate revolutionary zeal by encouraging challenges to established authority. It inflicted severe damage to the Chinese economy.

relationship to enter a new and more positive phase, particularly through economic co-operation. China presented greater problems. Japan loyally followed the United States in recognizing the Nationalist regime in Taiwan and came to derive much benefit from trade and investment in the island. But the Japanese government was cautious – or far-sighted – enough to resist Taiwanese pressure to block all contact with the Communist government in Beijing.

The Japanese attitude towards mainland China was complex. The turmoil and destruction caused by the 'Great Leap Forward' and 'Cultural Revolution' repelled many, even on the left-wing. Yet China was still admired as the source of Japan's own high culture and respected grudgingly as a nuclear power. Even more it was valued as a source of raw materials and a potentially vast market for Japanese goods. In fact, a low-profile trade was quietly developed, despite lack of official links between the two countries. By 1970 this accounted for about 2 per cent of Japan's exports and more than 20 per cent of China's imports.

Japanese attitudes towards the Soviet Union remained profoundly negative. A 1971 opinion poll amongst the general public revealed the USSR to be the most widely disliked foreign country in the world, ahead even of militaristic North Korea. Partly this reflected widespread anti-communism, partly memories of the brutal treatment of Japanese prisoners in Siberian camps after the war, and partly continued resentment at Russian occupation of the Kurile islands. Yet Japanese realism decreed that outright confrontation should be avoided. As far as possible Japan's policy was to be on good terms with all countries. Being virtually disarmed herself, she could plausibly claim to threaten no one. Besides, the USSR – as the world's second greatest military power – was a useful counterweight to China. And, rich in resources and backward in technology, it was potentially a great field of opportunity for Japanese industry. So both countries were content to allow their relationship to mark time.

Deprived of military muscle, hesitant in its diplomacy, Japan felt most confident internationally when dealing with matters of economy and technology. Much official energy, therefore, was devoted to the organization of Expo '70 at Osaka – an international exhibition designed to show to the world just how far Japan had advanced in the quarter century since its defeat. The unexpected events of 1971, however, were to jolt Japan into realizing that it could not afford self-congratulation about its place in the world. America, the cornerstone of Japan's diplomacy, was to take two initiatives which were to take the Japanese government completely by surprise.

All we need now is visitors: Expo '70.

The first concerned America's deficit on its balance of trade. In an effort to close the gap between exports and imports, President Nixon decided to allow the dollar to fall in value against other currencies, including the yen, thus making foreign goods more expensive for Americans to buy. At the same time he slapped a ten per cent surcharge on all imports. As 35 per cent of Japan's exports went to America, this was a real blow. And, because the measures were taken without prior warning, let alone consultation, they were regarded as something of an insult, as well as a shock.

Japanese businessmen blamed the trade gap on American wage-rises unmatched by gains in productivity, on the unwillingness of American exporters to master the Japanese language and complex distribution system, and on over-spending on the Vietnam war. The Japanese government, however, concerned to preserve their 'special relationship', still agreed to revalue the yen and open the Japanese market to new categories of American goods. Despite this compliant response the imbalance of trade between the two countries was even worse in 1972 than it had been in 1971.

The second of the 'Nixon Shocks' was the sudden announcement in July 1971 that the American President would visit Peking in the following year. Privately the Japanese applauded this move, regarding America's support for tiny Taiwan against the giant People's Republic as hopelessly unrealistic. What annoyed the Japanese, however, was the fact that their Prime Minister was informed of this basic shift in foreign policy by their major ally three minutes before it was broadcast on TV.

In fact the Americans moved swiftly to calm Japanese fears. President Nixon had a personal meeting with Prime Minister Sato before visiting Peking and publicly announced that no agreement would be reached between America and China that would prejudice Japan's interests. The two leaders also agreed that the island of Okinawa, a key base for the American military, would revert to Japanese sovereignty on 15 May 1972, thus bringing to a final close the American Occupation of Japanese soil.

In September 1972 Sato's successor as Prime Minister, Tanaka Kakuei, followed Nixon to Peking to re-establish ties with the People's Republic of China. Taiwan responded by breaking its diplomatic links with Japan; but trade ties continued without serious interruption, being too valuable to the Taiwanese to forego. Tanaka had begun his term of office well but the new year was to bring him – and Japan – a much sterner test and an even greater shock from quite another quarter.

A new beginning. Chairman Mao Zedong welcomes Prime Minister Tanaka to his home, September 1972.

5 INTO UNCERTAINTY 1973~80

Oil Shock

Also known as the 'Yom Kippur' war because Egypt launched its attack while Israel was observing the sacred 'Day of Atonement'.

In October 1973 a fourth war broke out in the Middle East between Israel and its Arab neighbours. As a direct result the Organization of Petroleum Exporting Countries (OPEC), which was dominated by Arab states, decided to limit the amount of oil some nations could buy and later to quadruple its price. OPEC's intention was to show support for the Arab cause by bringing economic pressure to bear on oil-importing industrial countries which were felt to be too favourable to Israel, rather than the Palestinians – on whose behalf the war was ostensibly being fought.

The 'oil shock' at once exposed Japan's extreme vulnerability to outside pressure. In 1941 it was a threat to her oil supplies which had prompted Japan's attack on Pearl Harbor. And the amount of oil used by Japan in 1941 wouldn't have been enough to keep the country going for even a week by the 1970s. The massive development of heavy industry and mass transportation, and of air-conditioning and other domestic conveniences, had brought with it a crucial dependence on outside suppliers of energy – which is the most basic requirement of a modern industrial economy. Japan depended on oil for about three-quarters of her energy needs and an overwhelming proportion of this came from the Middle East.

Japan's attack on the American naval base at Pearl Harbor on 7 December 1941, provoked the US declaration of war.

The impact of the oil embargo and price-hike was both immediate and long-lasting, a milestone in Japan's post-war history. The era of 'miracle growth' at around ten per cent per year came to a sudden halt. After a period of confused transition 'stable growth', at around 5 per cent per year, became the order of the day. The structure of industry was drastically changed and the pattern and sources of the nation's energy supplies substantially altered. In the end Japan was not only to survive but to prosper. And when a second 'oil shock' came in 1979, it was to be surmounted with relative ease.

But in the autumn and winter of 1973 this was all in the unguessable future. The government and people of Japan faced a crisis of unknown dimensions. Inflation had already begun to rise thanks to the new Prime Minister Tanaka's ambitious plans for 'Remodelling the Japanese Archipelago'. These plans were based on the assumption of ten per cent annual growth into the mid 1980s. The oil shock now made that assumption seem absurd and the 'Tanaka plan' was abruptly junked. Instead, a whole range of austerity measures was introduced to bring inflation under control, as manufacturers scrambled for oil and ordinary consumers scrambled for detergents and toilet paper, fearing that such everyday commodities might soon disappear from supermarket shelves.

Energy consumption was subject to new curbs, with limits on lighting in

Cracks in the miracle? Job-seekers reviewing prospects at a Tokyo unemployment centre.

Geothermal: energy derived from underground heat sources.

public places and rationing of fuel for industry and public alike. Hoarding fuel was treated as a criminal offence. Government itself set the example by introducing strict controls on lighting, heating and air-conditioning in offices and schools and hurriedly passing a 'Law for the Adjustment of the Oil Supply and Demand' and a 'Law for the Stabilization of the People's Livelihood'. Diplomatically, it tried to ease the pain by issuing statements of sympathy for the Palestinian cause – a matter about which few in official circles appear to have given much thought before.

1974 was a bad year for the Japanese economy. Business profits fell. Unemployment rose. The taboo on dismissing full-time workers meant that there were few outright redundancies but many part-timers, especially housewives, were sacked and few recruits were taken on. An estimated one third of the nation's industrial plant and equipment stood idle, killing any prospect of an economic revival through new investment. The slump was, of course, particularly bad in those industries most dependent on supplies of cheap oil; chemicals especially, but also building materials, lumber, paper and pulp, steel and shipbuilding and, to a lesser extent, textiles.

Economically, Japan sought salvation by a number of routes:
(A) Finding alternative suppliers of oil in North and South America, South-East Asia and as far away as Africa and the North Sea.
(B) Developing alternative sources of energy such as liquid natural gas, coal, solar, tidal, geothermal and nuclear power.
(C) Making energy-intensive industries, such as steel and cement, more efficient – or cutting back their capacity, as in chemicals and the refining of aluminium.
(D) Encouraging the rapid development of industries with lower energy requirements, such as machine tools, electronics or computers.
(E) Expanding service industries, like banking and retailing, to create new jobs.
(F) Controlling wage costs. Managements struggled to avoid outright sackings and in many cases set an example by taking pay cuts. In return workers accepted early retirement schemes, retraining and transfers out of unprofitable sectors in major companies, and lower wage rises – from an average 33 per cent in 1974, these fell to 13 per cent the following year, to nine per cent in 1976-7 and to six per cent in 1978-9. It is also important to note that Japanese workers did not use their large paper wage rise in 1974 to

increase their spending, which would have made inflation much worse. Instead, shaken by the crisis, they put it away for fear of a second shock and the need to have something extra to fall back on. This also helped greatly to cut inflation.

As a result of these efforts, manufacturing productivity in Japanese industry rose by an average 8.4 per cent between 1975 and 1978. This was not the result of investment in new equipment. Japan had too much lying idle and much was being scrapped. Rather, it was the result of spectacularly increased efficiency in the use of labour, energy and raw materials. Improvements in productivity rapidly restored Japan's competitiveness in international markets. While investment at home marked time, exports boomed again, rising from $56 billion in 1975 to $67.2 billion in 1976 and $80.5 billion in 1977. Eighty per cent of the increase was accounted for by cars and electrical goods. From 1975 onwards the balance of payments was back in surplus. By 1979 industry was operating at 90 per cent of its 1970 level. But export success brought its own problems, with growing trade friction with the United States and Europe, which resented the ever-widening gap between what they bought from Japan and what Japan bought from them.

Then came the 1979 revolution in Iran, which overthrew the rule of the Shah, Reza Pahlavi II, installed an 'Islamic' regime and prompted a second price-hike by OPEC. At the end of 1978, oil was $8 a barrel, by June 1979 $19, and by the beginning of 1980 $30. Drawing on the hard-won experience of 1973-5, the Japanese government made skilful use of taxes and limits on public spending to bring inflation down from 17.7 per cent in 1980 to 1.4 per cent in 1981. Japanese business, with equal skill and speed, cut back oil imports from 281,000,000 kilolitres in 1979 to 212,000,000 kilolitres in 1982. In strong contrast to the first oil crisis there was no confusion and little hoarding or speculation. Against this roller-coaster background Japanese standards of living continued to rise. The real income of a worker's household did actually fall by 0.3 per cent in 1974, but between 1975 and 1979 it rose by an average 2 per cent per year. Another slight fall in 1980 was followed by a similar resumption of modest growth, reflected in the increasing ownership of cars and air-conditioning, increased personal savings and increased expenditure on eating out – not to mention increased life expectancy.

Source A
Kosaka Masataka, an expert in international politics, analyses the oil crisis and suggests some possible responses:

We all know Japan is now facing a trial. However, its nature is not necessarily very clear . . . .

In the first place, we must note it was the first true 'crisis' experienced by Japan since the end of World War II. The world has had a number of crises in recent years. Wars have been fought in many places. However, none of these . . . have produced a direct impact on Japan; that is, they have not dealt a direct blow to Japan, who could remain an onlooker. The oil crisis represents the first time that Japan has felt the impact of a crisis squarely . . . .

Secondly, the crisis showed how vulnerable Japan's position is in the present world situation. The prospect of a 20 per cent cutback in the crude oil supply to Japan nearly paralyzed the Japanese economy and made us realize our weakness caused by dependence upon overseas natural resources . . .

In the future the oil producing countries will increase their petroleum production to a certain extent, but not enough to meet all of the increased demand for oil, and they will accumulate a considerable amount of foreign exchange, causing advanced industrial nations to be plagued by balance of payments difficulties. Under these circumstances, Japan will be unable to continue her 'high economic growth' either because she will not be able to procure enough oil or because she will not be able to expand her exports sufficiently to earn the huge amount of foreign exchange needed to pay for the oil imports . . . . Looking back through history, it must be admitted that Japan's fast economic growth since the end of World War II has been due not only to the capabilities of the Japanese people, but also to favourable

Tokai Mura, Japan's largest nuclear power plant. The 'nuclear option' was not a popular one.

international circumstances, especially the fact that she could almost endlessly expand her foreign trade and freely purchase resources . . . . In fact, a cool-headed review of last year's crisis will show that the existence of the crisis itself indicated the possibility of our survival. The Arab states lifted their oil embargo on Japan much earlier than expected . . . . The basic reason was that it had become clear that an economic blow to Japan would cause an even greater blow to many other countries. For instance, a decline in fertilizer production in Japan was bound seriously to affect agriculture in many other Asian countries. From this point of view, it may be said Japan has a certain type of power which arises from her capacity to serve other nations. Roughly speaking, this means that we must produce what foreign countries are seeking . . . .

Japan should contribute to the development of the techniques and institutions needed to produce resources. For instance, changing her own institutions to prevent excessive consumption of energy. We should increase our capacity to deal with emergencies by building up stockpiles. . . . Judging from what is now becoming clear, the cutoff in oil supply to Japan was not of the magnitude that would have given us a serious blow. The main issue is that we were unprepared. The capacity for economic growth must assume only secondary importance. To gain the ability to deal with various different situations will probably mean that we have reached 'maturity'.

Source B
Abe Yoko, a Japanese marketing consultant, describes the emergence of a new 'leisure class'. From 'Katei cho'ni natta onna tachi', *Shokun*, August 1979.

Calligraphy: the art of beautiful hand writing.

Koto: a harp-like musical instrument.

An explosion in leisure activities is taking place in present-day Japan. The numerous hobbies and recreational pursuits of a sample of fewer than 30 housewives between the ages of 35 and 43 bear this out. These women engage in all manner of sports-related activities: mountain climbing, tennis, riding, yoga, and practising for their driver's licences. They participate in cultural activities that include composing verses, joining reading circles, creative writing groups, they take exams to re-enter university or study for official English-language examinations, and join in political activities, they attend classical music concerts, plays, exhibitions. These women also work to acquire various skills . . . baking . . . studying Chinese and French cuisine . . . doing embroidery . . . and studying calligraphy, the koto, dressmaking and pottery. On the social scene, these women hold surprise parties, eat out on liberal budgets, go dancing and drinking, leaving their children at home. In a more practical vein they take courses . . . and undertake on-the-job training with the aim of establishing their own private businesses; they work part-time in local shops; they take correspondence courses, they undertake work on contract for clothing factories . . . .

Education for leisure: Japanese housewives experiment with new recipes.

Go: a game of strategy played with black and white counters on a squared board.

PTA: Parent Teacher Association.

. . . but what of their husbands? . . . 39.6 per cent said they enjoy gardening . . . 28.4 per cent play the traditional games of 'go' and Japanese chess, 20.9 per cent enjoy listening to records and 17.5 per cent keep pets. Compared to the explosion of leisure activities among women, this list is meagre. Men's leisure activities are indoor and retiring in nature, in dramatic contrast to the active and outgoing nature of their wives' interests in sports, culture, hobbies, social events and practical activities . . . .

The chief beneficiaries of Japan's high economic growth have been these housewives. Their husbands have sacrificed their holidays and relinquished their active participation in family affairs. And who has profited from this? The women.

The Japanese housewife has been inundated with countless electrical household appliances; her husband earns a salary that ranks among the highest in the world; and nuclearization of the family has freed her from the major task of caring for elderly parents. With all these innovations, something is amiss if a housewife does not have spare time. In a sense spare time is affluence. Japan's adult males, the counterparts of these housewives whose lives have been changed so dramatically by the growing independence of their children, were the target of a recent survey that revealed clearly the men's positon within the household.

Women are most often in control of the family purse strings. Only 32 per cent of the men said that they control the family assets. The education and discipline of children is discussed jointly by 51.7 per cent of the men; 41 per cent replied that the wife takes sole responsibility, and only 4.7 per cent said they assume responsibility themselves.

In PTA or neighbourhood community meetings, the participation of the wives is 79.1 per cent and 61.4 per cent respectively; husbands joining in . . . number only 17.8 per cent. Overall, wives outweigh husbands in their control of the house, household affairs, the family, the children and civic matters . . . . Today's middle-aged men are no longer the heads of their households. Their wives, with their long experience as consumers, their abundant free time and their assets and income to look after, now stand at the helm as the managers of Japan's households.

???

1 How far do you think successive Japanese governments can be blamed for the impact of the 1973 oil crisis on Japan?

2 How far were the recommendations of the author of Source A carried out? How accurate were his predictions?

3 In what ways do you think the lives of farmers' wives might be different from those of the housewives described in Source B?

4 Which aspects of the life-style in Source B would a Japanese housewife of the 1930s find most strikingly different to her own?

5 Why might Japanese wives have more leisure than their counterparts in the west?

Party Games

During the war all Japan's political parties were dissolved and merged together into a so-called 'Imperial Rule Assistance Association', which was politically more or less meaningless but was supposed to act as a sort of supporters' club for the militarist regime.

Under the Occupation real political parties re-emerged again. The most important were, on the left, two 'progressive' parties – the Socialists (JSP) and the Communists (JCP) and, on the right, two conservative groupings, the Liberals and the Democrats.

A Socialist-led coalition briefly held power in 1947 and a Democrat-led coalition in 1948; but thereafter power passed to the Liberals, led by Yoshida Shigeru, while the Socialists, the main opposition party, split into two factions.

Yoshida's fall in 1954 was followed by a brief phase of Democrat rule. However, when the two halves of the JSP re-united in 1955, the two conservative groupings merged in self-protection against this new challenge. The newly-created Liberal Democratic Party (LDP) was to rule Japan from then onwards.

Appealing to the people? Politicians continued to rely on mobilizing support through personal contact as well as the mass media.

Sokka Gakkai: the largest of the 'New Religions', which combines basically Buddhist rituals and beliefs with Christian forms of organization and methods of mission.

Although the 1960s saw the establishment of a major new party, Komeito ('Clean Government Party') by a religious movement Soka Gakkai ('Value Creating Society'), and an increased vote for the Communists, especially in rapidly growing cities, there was no serious challenge to LDP rule at national level. At municipal and prefectural level left-wing candidates could and did take power by campaigning on environmental issues; but the LDP took the hint and headed off their challenge by tackling environmental and welfare issues seriously.

The nation forged ahead through a decade of 'miraculous' economic growth and Prime Minister Sato Eisaku held power for almost eight years uninterrupted, retiring in 1972 to collect the Nobel Prize for Peace for his forthright opposition to nuclear weapons. In retrospect this period was to look like a 'golden era' for the conservatives.

Sato's resignation obliged the LDP to choose a new party president who would, by definition, as leader of the majority party in the National Diet, also be Prime Minister. There were four candidates, each with his own faction of party supporters in the Diet – Tanaka Kakuei, Miki Takeo, Fukuda Takeo and Ohira Masayoshi. Each was eventually to serve as Prime Minister in the course of the 1970s.

The 1972 leadership contest ended in victory for Tanaka, who soon sealed his triumph by visiting Beijing to re-establish Japanese diplomatic relations with the People's Republic of China. As a conservative politician Tanaka was very unusual. Most came from prosperous families and were university-educated. Tanaka came from a poor family, had only a basic education and made his way to a fortune through the building trade. He impressed voters and journalists alike as a tough, shrewd, no-nonsense man, a go-getter with the common touch. No one was surprised when he announced that his motto in office would be 'Decisiveness and Action'. His ambitious plan for 'Remodelling the Japanese Archipelago', however, started off a rapid rise in land prices as speculators bought up sites thought likely to benefit from government-backed development. Then in the autumn of 1973 came the 'oil shokku' to add a further vicious kick to the spiral of inflation.

As the Japanese economy appeared to be lurching towards chaos, Tanaka tried to shore up his support in the elections for the Upper House of the Diet in July 1974. This involved such a reckless use of election funds that Miki and Fukuda resigned from the Cabinet in protest. When the prestigious monthly magazine *Bungei Shunju* carried a long article on 'Tanaka Kakuei – His Money and His Men', exposing a wide range of corrupt practices, public outrage forced Tanaka to resign, though he remained the leader of a large personal faction within the party and thus a power behind the scenes.

In February 1976 a second scandal broke, also involving Tanaka, when it was alleged that he and other leading politicians had received millions of dollars in bribes from the American aircraft manufacturer Lockheed, who were trying to sell fleets of their planes to Japanese airlines. Tanaka's successor, the upright Miki, declined to protect him, though this was interpreted by some as vindictiveness and, after Tanaka was arrested, Fukuda and Ohira jointly called on Miki to step down. Meanwhile, six LDP members ostentatiously left the party to dissociate themselves from the scandal and established a separate grouping – the New Liberal Club.

With the ruling party in such turmoil it was hardly surprising that it lost support in the general election of December 1976. For the first time since 1967 the LDP failed to win 50 per cent of the vote and was only able to hold on to its majority in the lower house by successfully inviting a few newly-elected independent Diet members to join the party. Miki took the responsibility for the party's poor performance and finally resigned as leader. Fukuda was designated Prime Minister by a single vote and found himself

Ohira Masayoshi.

facing an opposition which, when it could combine, almost matched the strength of the governing party. The 'golden age' of conservative dominance had given way to an era of confusion and uncertainty.

Fukuda's main success in office was to sign a Treaty of Peace and Friendship with the People's Republic of China in 1978. He also established a new system whereby the president of the LDP, once elected, would hold office for only two years before having to submit himself for re-election. Ironically, in the first contest held under the new system, Fukuda himself was defeated by Ohira. Their conflict weakened the party and in the general election of October 1979 the LDP again suffered losses.

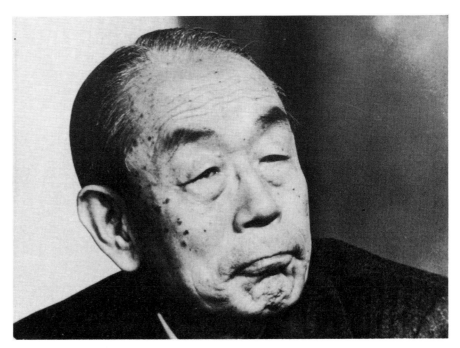

Fukuda Takeo.

So great was the rivalry between Ohira and Fukuda that the LDP was unable to reach agreement about who should be Prime Minister. In an unprecedented move it therefore passed the decision over to the Diet itself. Once again Ohira emerged triumphant, though by a narrow margin and after a second vote. Victory brought no harmony and Ohira's second term of office was to be short-lived. In May 1980 the opposition put forward a motion of no-confidence in the government. The Fukuda and Miki factions deliberately stayed away from the vote, the motion was passed and Ohira had no option but to dissolve the Diet and call another election.

The prospects for the LDP looked uncertain indeed after almost a decade of scandals and in-fighting. But the sudden death of Ohira just ten days before polling day appears to have shaken the LDP candidates into a semblance of unity and prompted an unexpected wave of sympathy among the electorate, which brought the LDP a landslide victory and a stable majority. Consultations within the party led to the emergence of a compromise candidate for the premiership in the person of Suzuki Zenko. In the light of the recent history of the party it was highly appropriate that he should choose as his motto 'Politics of Harmony'.

Japan entered the 1980s under the guidance of a political party which had held power continuously for a quarter of a century and appeared to be more firmly in control than ever, despite vicious squabbling and the taint of corruption. Why was this so?

One reason given by commentators was the fairly straightforward explanation that, whatever its imperfections, the LDP had delivered what the voters basically wanted most – an ever-rising standard of living and a foreign policy based on avoiding risks. Most voters, it was argued, simply did not wish to rock the boat.

Another explanation was the simple lack of alternatives, or rather the fact that there were too many alternatives in theory and none in practice. There seemed to be no realistic hope of forming a workable combination of centre or left-wing parties which could put itself foward as a credible coalition government. Any feasible coalition would have to include the Socialists because they were by far the biggest opposition party. But support for the Socialists had been eroding, partly at least, because trade unions, which provided the bulk of Socialist supporters, were themselves losing members as Japan's industrial structure changed – rendering the older, more highly unionized industries less and less important. The Socialist party proved quite unable to forge a stable pattern of alliances with other groups. If it agreed a compromise programme with the Communists it would only do so at the cost of losing the support of the centre parties – and vice versa. The JSP was, moreover, burdened with a tradition of pseudo-revolutionary language which frightened people – and Marxist approaches to problems, which alienated them. More and more people saw it as outdated, unrealistic, or simply irrelevant to Japan's future as it appeared to be unfolding. Finally, the militant pacifism which had for so long attracted voters to the Socialist cause had lost its appeal as memories of the war faded, acceptance of the Self-Defence Force became widespread, and tensions caused by growing Soviet military power caused more and more people to regard a call for 'unarmed neutrality' as positively irresponsible.

Source A

A Tokyo University Professor analyses how Japanese political parties organize support. From Prof. Sato Seizaburo, 'Kiro ni tatsu Jiminto seiken', *Chuo Kuron*, July 1983.

Constituency: body of voters who elect a representative.

At the time of its formation the LDP was very poorly organized both in fund raising and in its ability to marshal pressure groups and was largely dependent on the individual ties of factional leaders for its organizational strength. Since the major constituencies of the old nonsocialist parties had been the traditional sectors of farming villages and the old urban middle class, the early LDP was strongly tradition-oriented . . . . By interceding with the . . . . government on behalf of their constituencies and influencing the way public works investments, government subsidies and other public funds were distributed, LDP Diet members built their own support associations into efficient vote-gathering machines . . . . The LDP's success stands in marked contrast to the failure of the Socialist Party, which, as the permanent opposition party, limited its organizational base to trade unions.

High economic growth did not always work in the LDP's favour . . . the massive exodus of people from the country to the city resulted in the emergence of large numbers of voters who could not be brought under the wing of support associations. Nor could the majority of these voters be brought under the wing of organizations sympathetic to the Socialists. [Many were, or were employed by, owners of small businesses who were hostile to unions.] The LDP, like the JSP, consistently lost ground in cities in terms of the percentage of the vote obtained. The parties that succeeded to some extent in organizing the urban voters that the LDP and the JSP failed to capture, were first the Komeito and next the Communist Party, after it repudiated its violent revolution policy in 1958. This is why these two parties made such remarkable gains in the 1960s and the beginning of the 1970s.

? ?

1 What does the source suggest about the way in which support for parties is affected by (a) opportunities to make personal contact with candidates (b) population movement (c) the structure of the labour force?

2 For what purposes do political parties need an organization?

The Defence Debate

The National Police Reserve (75,000 men), established at MacArthur's bidding in August 1950 against the background of the outbreak of war in Korea, was soon upgraded and retitled to become the National Safety Force (110,000 men) and in 1954, the Self-Defence Force (SDF) (146,000 men), with Ground, Air and Maritime units.

Japan's first Post-War statement on basic defence policy was issued in 1957, pledging the country to:

. . . gradually improve its defence power to make it more efficient within the necessary limits of self-defence in accordance with national power and conditions.

In other words, Japan would assume a limited measure of responsibility for its own defence, but very gradually and only in so far as it could afford to. This cautious approach was justified on a number of grounds:

(a) The memory of defeat and its accompanying poverty and national humiliation was still strong and so therefore was suspicion of the military, who were held directly responsible for the disaster, having usurped the power of civilian governments in the 1930s and plunged into the invasion of China. The Socialist and Communist parties were especially virulent in their attacks on anything that looked like a resurgence of militarism or an attempt to alter the 'peace clause' – Article 9 – of the constitution. Many left-wing thinkers went further, calling for totally 'unarmed neutrality', arguing that since Japan intended only peaceful relations with other countries, it was unthinkable that any other country would attack her.

(b) Rearmament would alarm Japan's neighbours in East and South East Asia who had suffered at the hands of Japanese forces. Thus, far from contributing to regional security, Japanese rearmament would 'de-stabilize' the area.

(c) Rearmament would involve higher taxes and divert investment funds away from further industrial expansion.

Japan therefore continued to rely on the 'American umbrella'. Successive governments also pledged themselves to uphold 'three non-nuclear principles' – not to produce or possess nuclear weapons or to allow such weapons to be brought on to Japanese soil. But they also proclaimed their support for American forces in Vietnam – while reassuring the public that the SDF would *never* be sent to operate overseas. They also took care not to enquire too closely whether visiting American ships were, in fact, carrying nuclear weapons. (When US Ambassador Reischauer later (1981) revealed that American ships putting into Japanese ports did carry nuclear weapons as a matter of routine, the Japanese government duly expressed its shock, surprise and dismay.)

In 1970 the Japanese government's White Paper, reformulated in the light of the renewal of the 1960 Security Treaty, set out the nation's defence priorities by pledging that:

Japan is a great power economically but it will not become a great power militarily. Rather it will become a new kind of state with social welfare and world peace as its goals.

In the same year, however, the new Director-General of the Defence Agency, Nakasone Yasuhiro, commissioned a study of Japan's defence system, which would enable the country to become more self-reliant. This study proposed a new approach – that invasion forces should not be resisted 'at the water's edge' but intercepted on the high seas, which would have involved a

Don't refer to it as the army! The Ground Self-Defence Force on parade.

considerable strengthening of Japan's air and sea forces. In the event the plan was dropped after strong opposition in the Diet.

After the re-establishment of Japanese relations with China in 1972 the opposition argued that any further build-up of Japanese forces was quite unnecessary, because a threat from Beijing was no longer possible. Other voices on the left argued that Japan's defence needs should be met by a UN force ('just in case'). They did not explain how the UN could actually do that, which nations would be willing to release their troops for such service or why, indeed, any should want to. Yet other critics suggested Japan should place its faith in resisting an invader by means of a general strike and other forms of civilian resistance.

On the other hand, the USSR continued to build up its military strength, particularly on the high seas. And, from 1973 onwards, the Americans pulled their troops out of Vietnam. Following on the 'Nixon shocks' of 1971 this raised a very uncomfortable question in Japanese minds: would the Americans really come to Japan's aid in a crisis? Defence remained a matter of concern and uncertainty throughout the 1970s. In September 1976 the pilot of a Soviet MiG-25 landed at Hakodate, Hokkaido and asked for political asylum. A furore erupted when it was revealed that Japan's surveillance system had, at one point, completely lost track of the plane. Japan's air defences were suddenly exposed as far less efficient than had been supposed.

Furore broke out again in July 1978 when General Kurisu, chairman of the Joint Staff Council, responsible for overall command of Japan's SDF, remarked in a newspaper interview that in the event of an emergency, it might be impossible for a front-line commander to consult his political masters before taking action. This led to an immediate political storm and accusations that military leaders were flaunting the principle of civilian control. Was this a warning that the military arrogance of the 1930s was still alive?

Not at all. Kurisu bowed to the storm and resigned. General Takashina readily accepted the invitation of the Prime Minister to take his place. (It had been a standard tactic of the pre-war military to refuse to serve under civilian politicians whose policies they disapproved of.) Fukuda did, however, authorize a review of the legal position covering military responses to emegencies. Even this provoked the JSP and JCP to charge that the government was seeking to strengthen the authority of the military.

A quarter of a century after the establishment of Japan's Post-War defence forces there was still no fundamental agreement among the political parties about their role. Nor was the public any more at ease. A poll conducted by the *Asahi Shimbun* newspaper in 1978 found that while a majority (57 per cent) favoured maintaining the SDF at its present level, an even larger majority (71 per cent) opposed changing the Constitution to enable Japan to keep a full-scale military establishment. And while 42 per cent said a peaceful fogeign policy was Japan's best protection, only 2 per cent relied on the SDF. More than half (54 per cent) said that they did not think Japan would be attacked by a foreign country, but more than half (56 per cent) also thought that if it was America would not come to Japan's aid. Meanwhile, the SDF had grown to become 240,000 strong, with 150 ships and 1000 aircraft. In defence spending, although this was limited to a ceiling of one per cent of GNP, Japan by 1979 ranked as the ninth greatest military power in the world.

The defence spending limit of one per cent was only a matter of convention, not of law.

Source A
Nakasone Yasuhiro, a future Prime Minister, proposes new thinking about Japan's defence and calls for constitutional revision.

Periphery: boundary.

If a part of town is left uninhabited, weeds spring up, snakes infest it and mosquitoes breed and it soon becomes a garbage dump. To create a military vacuum is to create the maximum danger of inviting precisely such a situation. In this sense, it is the international duty and responsibility of every nation in today's world to establish and maintain a balance on its periphery with the minimum defence power necessary to deter other nations from entertaining aggressive ambitions and urges. What are the most irresponsible attitudes in the international community? Militarism is one and unarmed neutrality is the other. Unarmed neutrality is a concept condoning negligence of one's own self-defence within the international community. This is a point of view that fails to understand the nature of one's own duty . . . . The ideas concerning demilitarization heard in certain academic quarters in Japan and smug assertions of the right of peaceful survival are idle arguments that would be ridiculed in the real world of international politics . . . . When I was Minister of International Trade and Industry, I had the opportunity to visit China. During my conversations with Zhou Enlai, he referred to Chairman Mao Zedong as having remarked that the Japan Socialist Party was a very 'strange political party'. Chairman Mao was quoted as having said, 'They don't defend their own country. Only a mentally deranged person would advocate unarmed neutrality and the like. What a strange political party.'

According to a public opinion survey . . . support for the SDF has reached approximately 83 per cent of the population. Asked whether the SDF violates the Constitution 48 per cent answered no and 20 per cent yes, while 30 per cent were not sure . . . . Accordingly, we can assume that the Japanese people have approved the SDF as the minimum defence capability necessary for the protection of Japan and that this line of thought has now taken root. . . . Furthermore, since it is a historical fact that the present Constitution was drawn up based on occupation policy at a time when the Japanese did not have complete free will, review is also warranted from the standpoint of a democratic constitution.

? ?

1 In what ways do you think Nakasone's argument shows the impact of the 1973 oil crisis on Japan?

2 Why do you think Nakasone included the anecdote about the attitude of Chairman Mao Zedong?

6 WHICH WAY NEXT?
1980s AND BEYOND

Being Japanese

In May 1977 the Japanese government announced that Japan had passed the point in time at which more than 50 per cent of the population had been born since the War. This prompted the information technology expert Masuda Yoneji to attempt to define the distinctive characteristics of the Post-War Japanese. He came to the conclusion that

people of this generation are basically different from their predecessors . . . they are westernized Japanese with a sense of individualism and a scientific outlook . . . they know neither war nor hunger and, most important . . . they are ignorant of the oppression of authority . . . . Exaggerating a bit, we can say that the first Post-War generation has developed a semi-Americanized way of thinking and living.

Masuda characterized Japan's post-war generation, then in their early thirties, as the MEC generation. M stood for 'motorization', which, to him, meant being mobile and also aware of being a member of an advanced nation with a high standard of living. E stood for English; knowing at least something of the language and the culture of English-speaking peoples, being open to international influences and values, and being relaxed in the company of foreigners. C meant computers, which implied to Masuda familiarity with hi-tech and also the ability to gather information independently and to think about it critically. Masuda saw this generation of new Japanese as optimistic, outgoing and flexible. What worried him was whether, never having known hardship and seemingly separated from their own national traditions, they might 'lack the spiritual strength to weather the storms of national crisis'. And what of the teenagers? A variety of surveys conducted around 1980 revealed that:

(a) They were getting bigger. Between 1948 and 1978, thanks largely to improved nutrition, the average height of 12-year-old boys had increased by 12 cms and of 14-year-olds by 17 cms. Tests showed, however, that they were not necessarily getting stronger. Indeed in strength, suppleness and speed of reaction the nation's youth actually seemed to be losing ground.

(b) They owned a lot of expensive possessions. 70 per cent of 14-year-olds had a watch and a portable cassette recorder/radio; 30 per cent had a camera; 20 per cent had a guitar, telescope, microscope or pocket calculator; 12 per cent had their own stereo set and 11 per cent their own TV.

(c) Most young people lived in cities, regarding the countryside merely as somewhere to visit.

(d) Very few children experienced the death of a parent before they had

In 1985 the Japanese were eating more meat (up 5 per cent from 1970) but less cereals (down 9 per cent over the same period).

In 1987 there were 11 cities in Japan with a population greater than one million.

Jamericans? Japanese children at school lunch – casual clothes, bread and milk, and no chopsticks.

themselves grown up. This was in strong contrast to the 1930s when younger children were often orphaned by the early death of parents.

(e) Because of the trend to small families, most children had one brother or sister or none at all; and most lived apart from their grandparents.

(f) The decline in the number of small family businesses meant that fewer and fewer children saw their home as also being a place of work.

Compared with their grandparents, these children lived lives which were highly affluent, urbanized, mobile and rich in information and novelty. Controlled for more hours over more years at school, they were, however subject to much looser discipline at home.

If the experiences of Japan's post-war generations are distinctive so also are those of their grandparents. A significant by-product of Japan's post-war economic success has been a dramatic increase in life-expectancy, which in turn has meant that the population of Japan contains an ever-growing proportion of people over 65. Japanese have become greatly concerned with the implications of their 'greying society'. What will it mean in terms of the demand for pensions, medical care and specialized housing and recreational facilities? Accounting for 8.6 per cent of the population in 1978, the over 65s were predicted to increase as a proportion of the population by 2.8 per cent per year until by the year 2020 they would reach 19 per cent of the total. In 1980 a 'Society of Families Supporting Senile Old People' was established. Was this a portent of the future?

A comparative survey, conducted for the Prime Minister's office in 1980, did suggest that in many ways old people in Japan were better treated than in Britain or the USA:

(a) Over half of the respondents in Japan lived with their married children – less than 10 per cent did in the United States or Britain. In Japan only 6 per cent lived alone – in Britain and the US over 40 per cent did so.

(b) In Japan over 40 per cent of the respondents were still working. The comparable figure for the USA was 24 per cent and for Britain 8 per cent.

(c) In Japan some 30 per cent of respondents received money regularly from their children – in the two western countries virtually none did. And in Japan only 14 per cent considered themselves hard up, whereas in Britain 18 per cent did and in the US 28 per cent.

The Japanese have been aware of the onset of the 'greying society' for some time and are concerned to make a positive response to the challenge – above

Keeping active. As the proportion of pensioners rises inexorably, the question is raised – what are they to do?

Many Japanese do *technically* retire at 55. Most of these continue to work, at least part-time.

all by making the 'autumn years' of retirement a happy and fulfilling experience. But this is no easy task for a generation which lived through depression and war and, during the years of reconstruction, was constantly called upon to work, work, work. There is a danger that, divorced from work and their friends at work, such people might feel rootless and useless. And, with the increased use of robots and computers at work, the likelihood is that the retirement age will rapidly be lowered from 65 to 60 or even 55. The problem of 'ikigai' – a purpose to life – will become that much more acute. In 1978 therefore, Mitsubishi Electric introduced its 'Silver Plan' – a programme designed to help workers over 40 begin organizing their lives towards retirement. In 1980 Musashino City, in the Tokyo area, introduced a new system whereby old people with a house or land but no close relatives could receive meals and care in return for leaving their property to the city after their death.

Apart from the urgent need to develop new social institutions suited to an ageing society, it is also interesting to note that 'Japanese researchers also see the further rapid development of computers and robots as even more essential if Japan is to produce the wealth needed to sustain an aged population in comfort from an active working population which will be 20 per cent smaller than it is today'.

Ever since the armed intrusion of advanced western powers in the mid-nineteenth century Japan has, in one way or another, been obsessed with 'catching up with the West'. Now, in wealth, health and technology, it has done so and has itself become a front-runner. 'Japanese inventiveness' might have seemed a contradiction in terms half a century ago, when the Japanese were renowned for their 'copycat' approach to modern industry. Now, striking new developments in such fields as robotics, lasers, computers, 'mechatronics', ceramics and biotechnology are eagerly awaited from Japanese researchers.

As far back as 1979 an American survey revealed how far other countries were behind Japan in the use of industrial robots – 47,000 were already at work in Japan, compared with less than 6000 in West Germany, just over 3000 in the USA and under 200 in Britain. Japan, moreover, had 135 companies

Factories without workers? Welding robots in action 1984.

producing robots and 80 laboratory teams researching their development. All this since 1967, when the first robot had been imported from the United States. By 1970 Kawasaki Heavy Industries had produced Japan's first robot. By 1980 Fujitsu had opened a plant where robots manufactured robot parts – which were still assembled by humans. The robot-made robot had not yet arrived but it was on its way. Robots work tirelessly and not only release humans from tedious and repetitive tasks but also from working in environments which are dark, dusty, dirty or noisy. Within limits, these do not bother a robot. And robots make possible immense improvements in productivity. In Odawara City, near Tokyo, a small company manufactures the heads for disposable lighters. In 1979 its ten employees produced 900,000 units a day. In 1984 two supervisors and a team of robots were turning out four million a day.

Many Japanese, especially of the older generation, have expressed the fear that new technologies and western influences will between them make future generations careless of Japanese traditions. Writing in 1983, the sociologist Kato Hidetoshi observed reassuringly that some 70 million people had visited a shrine or temple on New Year's Day that year, according to ancient custom, a figure which had to include large numbers of young people. Moreover, he suggested, thanks to increased leisure and the opportunities afforded by longer schooling and company-sponsored education schemes, there were far more Japanese women practising ikebana (traditional flower-arranging) than there would have been half a century ago. Other examples of the persistence of tradition abound. Men wear western suits to the office but slip into a comfortable 'yukata' when they get home. Electric calculators are everywhere but more than a million people every year take the examinations organized by the Japan Chamber of Commerce and Industry to test expertise in the soroban (abacus). Japan adopted the metric system back in 1959 but Japanese still use traditional methods of measurement for clothes, furnishing and room sizes. And there are still more than 30,000 traditional fortune-tellers in business. Professor Kato argues that fears about the disappearance of tradition are based on a misunderstanding:

Tradition is alive and well. (Left) A matsuri (festival) means a get-together and letting off steam. (Right) Shinto rituals still prevail at weddings.

Source A
Umeshima Miyo, a Japanese businesswoman, foresees a bright future for women working with computers. From Umeshima Miyo, 'Pasokon wa OL tachi no kyusei shu?', *Voice*, September 1983.

. . . intellectuals have been dominated by the . . . assumption that modernization could be achieved only through the rejection of tradition. In my view, tradition and modernization are complementary, rather than contradictory . . . people now drive to shrines in their own cars and the women studying ikebana in factory classrooms assemble the most advanced electronics equipment at their work stations . . . Japan is a country that permits the harmonious co-existence of old and new. Japan's very existence and functioning have built upon this harmony.

We have reached the point where the fear that machines will rob humans of work can no longer be shrugged off . . . . The computer and software industry, however, seems to have a chronic shortage of workers and welcomes female employees . . . . The industry's statistics show that in 1981 the number of professional key punchers, computer operators and programmers exceeded 2 million and their number is growing more rapidly than that of men . . . .

I decided to investigate the state of professional female workers in this industry . . . . What these women said can be summarized as follows. First, they felt they were in a good working environment. Unlike other occupations, there was no pressure on them to behave in certain pre-defined womanly ways. Their work was evaluated for what it was worth. One of the pleasures was the refusal of the computers themselves to discriminate between men and women . . . . They also emphasized that programming requires patience . . . . Because women have traditionally been trained in handicraft skills, they gain abilities that can be put to good use with computers . . . .

Women who pride themselves on their brain-power and who thereby earn dislike at the normal company become well-adjusted workers in the computer business. When given a routine and repetitive task such women are liable to provoke resentment . . . . In this occupation . . . even women who are not quick to respond to others' needs or who are poor at teamwork can work free from care . . . .

. . . the disposition required of a female technician is a willingness and aptitude to undertake highly specialized work. Japanese women are well equipped in this regard. It was the vocational aptitude of women that supported the development of the textile industry, once Japan's leading industry, and women also sustained the subsequent development of the electrical appliance industry. Now the tireless handwork of women is being put to use in another frontline industry: computer software . . . . In the past, women were the textile experts, and they brought patience, perseverance and perfectionism to their work. Given this favourable tradition, we can expect women to be put to even better use in work with computers . . . . When the textile industry became male-dominated . . . women lost the opportunity to enjoy intellectual challenges. The software industry is still a new field, so the work is comparatively free . . . . This is also an occupation allowing working arrangements suited to women's lifestyle . . . . As workplaces closer to home proliferate and arrangements for working at home take shape, women will not be forced to neglect their children or to skimp their care of elderly parents . . . . the computer industry . . . will indeed bring revolutionary progress to the lives of working women. When I consider the inflexibility of Japan's male-dominated society, I feel hesitant as stating this so positively. But traditional patterns of dominance . . . have little relevance in the computer world.

New woman (right) – the first woman executive at Kanebo Cosmetics Masako Hosaka
(below) Doi Takako, the first woman to lead a major Japanese political party – the JSP from September 1986.

? ?

1 What does this source tell you about the way in which women are treated in other Japanese industries? How do you explain these attitudes?

2 Do you find this argument persuasive?

Being International

The Japanese are a great people. They cannot and should not be satisfied with a world role which limits them to making better transistor radios and sewing machines and teaching other Asians how to grow rice.

That, at least, was the opinion that Lee Kwan Yew, Prime Minister of Singapore, expressed to (the later President) Richard Nixon in 1965.

Few westerners at that time were taking the Japanese seriously. Some still treated them with outright contempt. General de Gaulle was widely reported to have referred to a Japanese Prime Minister as 'that transistor salesman'. And over a decade later, in the late 1970s, an EEC report was to refer slightingly to the Japanese as 'a nation of workaholics living in rabbit-hutches'. Such remarks were widely reported in Japan and served to confirm many Japanese in their view that foreigners were incapable of understanding or appreciating their achievements. The continued strength of this feeling may help to explain one of the enduring paradoxes of modern Japan.

For a society so open to foreign ideas, so eager to buy foreign luxuries, Japan in the 1980s was still curiously closed to foreign people, as a 'Survey on National Living Preferences', conducted by the Economic Planning Agency, revealed in 1986. While more than 70 per cent of respondents favoured increasing the volume of news, technology, mail, telephone calls, tourists and students from overseas, less than 30 per cent were in favour of more permanent or intimate contact with foreigners, as represented by foreign employees working in Japan or marriages between Japanese and non-Japanese. A similar 'Survey on Social Attitudes', conducted by the Prime Minister's Office in 1985 showed that almost 50 per cent of the Japanese were not even interested in becoming friends with a foreigner.

Japan's economic development has, however, made Japan a more international place, whatever the Japanese may think about it. The number of foreigners entering Japan rose to 2.3 million in 1985, an increase of eight times over the 1965 figure – but this was still less than one sixth of the number of people passing through Britain each year. The number of registered resident aliens in 1985 was 850,000, an increase of 180,000 since 1965; but 80 per cent of these were Japanese-speaking Koreans, who had migrated before or during the last war. The number of marriages between Japanese and non-Japanese reached 12,000 in 1985, three times the 1965 figure – but still only 1.7 per cent of the total number of marriages. The number of foreign students in Japan trebled between 1975 and 1985 to reach 18,000 – just 0.8 per cent of the total enrolled in higher education, compared with 4.7 per cent in the USA and 7.9 per cent in Britain. Many barriers prevent Japanese society becoming more international, apart from the general attitudes of the public. The high value of the yen makes Japan impossibly expensive for students unless they have special financial assistance. Official procedures involving the customs service, police and so on seem to be based on the assumption that foreigners are less an asset than a potential source of trouble. All resident aliens, for example, are required to be finger-printed, both when they land and every five years thereafter. Not until 1982, to take another example, could non-Japanese be offered permanent teaching posts at state universities. By 1987 there were 52 – out of 40,000.

Things *are* changing. Department stores like Seibu, which import many Western goods, have started hiring foreigners on a regular basis – and complaining about how much government paperwork getting work-permits involves. Honda, which sees itself as a global company rather than simply a Japanese one, is beginning to groom foreign recruits for senior management posts. The global nature of modern finance has pushed Fuji Bank in the same direction. And the Ministry of Education has pledged to raise the number of

Reluctant teacher? Technicians from developing countries come to Japan to learn new skills.

foreign students in Japan to 40,000 by 1992 and 100,000 by the year 2000. Perhaps most surprising of all is a development taking place in remote farming villages which, at first thought, one would expect to be the most socially conservative of all communities. Because they are losing so many young women to the comfortable life of the big cities, villagers are sending away for Filipino and Sri Lankan brides for the young men who will inherit family farms and remain tied to the village.

To a very great extent the issue of Japan's 'internationalization' in the 1980s revolved around the nature of its relations with the United States – its chief

Shoulder to shoulder. US President Ronald Reagan and Japanese Prime Minister Nakasone Yasuhiro.

ally, major customer and most important source of foreign ideas and technology. When Nakasone Yasuhiro became Prime Minister in 1982 observers saw the possibility of a significant step forward in Japanese-American relations. Nakasone was Japan's first English-speaking Prime Minister, and this was felt to open up the possibility of a closer and easier relationship with the American President, and thus with America itself. President Reagan's typically warm personal response to the new leader soon gave Japanese journalists the chance to refer to the 'Ron-Yas dialogue' as the two men conferred on first-name terms.

But relations between the two countries were soured by continuing friction over their ever-growing trade gap which, by 1984, had reached $37 billion in Japan's favour. In the American Congress representatives from manufacturing areas demanded tariff and quota protection against Japanese imports. Japanese manufacturers counter-charged that Americans did not make the necessary effort to penetrate the, admittedly difficult, but immensely profitable Japanese market. Further squabbles arose over American access to participation in Japan's stock exchange, in Japanese construction projects and in the development of Japan's telecommunications system. Economic issues seemed to develop a persistent tendency to become diplomatic rows, and Japan was obliged to make a series of gestures of appeasement. In 1985 Prime Minister Nakasone personally appeared on television to present an 'action programme' designed to boost imports. He appealed for every Japanese to buy at least $100 worth of imported goods – which would reduce Japan's trade surplus by $12 billion. But they didn't. In 1986 the Maekawa Report, issued by a high-powered team of businessmen and officials established at government initiative, recommended further major steps to open up the Japanese economy in order to assuage foreign criticism. But the surplus kept on rising.

In the autumn of 1985 the underlying strength of the Japanese economy was recognized by a hefty upward revaluation of the yen. Over the course of the succeeding two years it increased in value by 40 per cent against other major currencies, making Japanese exports that much dearer and imports that much cheaper. By 1988 this did appear to be having some effect on the trade surplus. It had also driven many small, export-based Japanese companies into bankruptcy. Japan's economic pre-eminence and the continuing problems of an America in which government and consumers alike were over-spending wildly, led some Japanese to ask much broader questions about the respective roles of the two countries in the future. The economist Nakatani Iwao argued that Japan must rouse itself to play a far more active role in the development of the international economy. Since 1945 world trade had expanded within a framework of rules and institutions, such as the International Monetary Fund and General Agreement on Tariffs and Trade, which had been devised by the USA – with America itself as the powerhouse of growth and major regulator of the system. Now America was visibly faltering, maintaining its high living-standards only by means of massive borrowing abroad – which had turned her into the world's largest debtor. And who was now the world's largest creditor? – Why, Japan, which in 1986 had exported capital to the value of $134 billions.

According to Nakatani, America would soon become too involved in sorting out its debt problems to be able to continue to stimulate world trade. Therefore Japan would have to take over this role. He foresaw a major obstacle, however, in the unwillingness of the Japanese to accept that Japan could only take the lead by making its own economy as open as America's had been. This would upset and disturb a whole range of powerful vested interests – rice farmers protected by tariffs, building firms and stockbrokers protected by regulations and small shopkeepers protected by the immense complexity of the distribution system.

Japan, Nakatani argued, faced a stark choice. She must either refuse to accept the pain of change and risk growing international resentment and protectionism – which would eventually push it into isolation and economic decline – or expose inefficient farmers and other protected groups to foreign competition, encourage imports and welcome the establishment of foreign companies on Japanese soil.

On the one side, therefore, there are those Japanese who argue that it is Japan's unique homogeneity that accounts for its social harmony and economic productivity. On the other there are those who point out that seventeenth-century Holland, nineteenth-century Britain and twentieth-century America gained immense vitality from the contributions of migrant peoples. Only by becoming more open to non-Japanese, they argue, can Japanese companies and universities expect to remain dynamic and in tune with a rapidly-changing world.

By the 1980s Japan's stature as an economic superpower was beyond question. The Japanese economy produced over ten per cent of the world's wealth – making Japan twice as big in economic terms as West Germany, the industrial powerhouse of Europe. Yet Japan accounted for only 2.6 per cent of the world's population and 0.3 per cent of its land area. The value of shares traded on the Tokyo Stock Exchange exceeded the value of those of London or New York. And in terms of real estate Japan was reckoned to be worth three times as much as the entire United States – which is 30 times larger. And while Japan by 1986 had only 12 of the world's largest manufacturing companies (measured by sales), compared with America's 48, she had seven of the world's top ten richest banks – and by 1988 all ten of them.

Ironically, the Japanese did not *feel* well off. While they could buy cars, appliances and other internationally traded goods at highly competitive prices, it was quite a different situation with goods which were not subject to international competition, either because in their nature they could not be traded (like housing, recreational facilities, power supplies or local transport) or because they were protected by tariffs, quotas or other regulations (like agricultural products, and especially rice). The Japanese were also conscious that not only was their country far less well provided than Western countries with such 'public goods' as parks and museums, but that they also worked on average about ten hours a week more than their European counterparts.

The sociologist Hayashi Kenjiro agreed with Nakatani that the crumbling of America's industrial leadership signalled the ending of an era in the history of the world order. But Japan, in his view, was unprepared to take over a position of world leadership. So steps should be taken to build the foundations for a new Japan-led world order. These would include:

(a) Upholding the doctrine of free trade, even if America resorted to protectionism, because free trade policies had produced the great post-war world trade boom, which had raised living-standards around the world.

(b) Making the yen *the* major international currency and accepting responsibility for managing the world monetary system.

(c) Making Tokyo *the* major centre for raising capital for development around the world.

But the most vital task, according to Hayashi, would not be economic but cultural – 'creating a system of education designed to create first-class international citizens is the most important long-term investment we can make.'

Hayashi's prescription is also a prediction:

Internationalization in action – a Japanese executive chairs a meeting at at Japanese-owned factory in the north-east of England.

The twenty-first century will see Japan exporting culture and information to the rest of the world; at that point the process of Japan's internationalization will be complete and the country will also have met the requirements for true

leadership in the world community. We Japanese must now decide how to go about creating, before the end of this century, a culture that we can be proud to offer to the world.

Source A
Takeuchi Hiroshi, chief economist at the Long-Term Credit Bank of Japan, suggests how Japan's wealth may shape its future. From 'Kakute kigyo wa 'tei seicho kokka' Nihon o dasshutsu suru', *Next*, March 1985.

. . . even with their new-found abundance, the Japanese remain as diligent savers as ever: about a quarter of GNP goes into savings. Given that less than this amount is invested by the private sector, where does the remainder go?

Much of it goes to the government, which uses it to build roads and the like . . . the government paves mountain roads that no one travels, builds museums in every little rural backwater, and adds libraries and cafeterias to elementary schools. It also lavishes funds on welfare and on the salaries of government workers . . . .

Yet even with the government siphoning off surplus savings to the point of bankrupting public finance, there are still some left. What happens to this excess? It is exported . . . .

Since there is no way Japan can use up the foreign currency it acquires . . . an equivalent sum flows overseas in the form of foreign investment. Thus both goods and capital are continually streaming out of the country. And the bulk of both flows ends up in the United States . . . . Ironically, we are aiding the growth of a country superior to ours in economic strength, technological resources and living standards. In return, we get bashed for our trade practices.

How has this situation come about? Why . . . are Japanese firms investing in the United States?

In Japan, if one wants to buy land to build a factory, the average cost is about ¥ 30,000 per square metre. In the South of the United States the cost of land is about ¥ 300 and labour is about the same as in Japan. At present some 7000 Japanese firms have advanced overseas in this manner.

This is not altogether a bad thing, of course. The spread of Japanese capital means the spread of Japanese culture, which is to be welcomed. Only by disseminating their culture and getting Westerners to recognize its value can Asians overcome their disadvantage in Western society. The flow of capital overseas assists this process.

In the United States today even the smaller cities have Japanese restaurants . . . . IBM's main office in New York has a Japanese-style garden . . . . Americans have begun to take Japanese-style baths . . . . Knowledge of the language has spread to the extent that it is no longer safe to insult someone in Japanese on the streets of New York. All this, of course, enhances Americans' understanding of Japanese culture and that is an excellent thing.

What will be the effect on Japan if this trend continues? For one thing, Japanese firms will become progressively multinational in character. For another, the returns on current investments will eventually find their way back to Japan. Ultimately we will be able to live on the interest. Free of factories on its own soil and living graciously on high returns from its overseas investments, Japan will become a beautiful country . . . . then culture will truly flower. A flowering culture and a wilting economy: this is the direction in which Japan is headed.

? ?

1 What other reasons, apart from cheap land, are there for Japanese industry to re-locate abroad?

2 Does the author of the Source approve of the current management of the Japanese economy? What alternatives might he suggest?

3 Do you think he means his predictions seriously?

JAPAN
YEAR BY YEAR
SINCE 1945

1945 Fire-bombing of Tokyo. Fall of Okinawa. A-bomb destruction of Hiroshima and Nagasaki.
Surrender of Japan following Emperor's first-ever broadcast.
Occupation begins. Demobilization of Japanese forces.

1946 New Year's Day broadcast – Emperor renounces divine status.
Showa constitution announced.
Women vote for the first time.

1947 Showa constitution comes into force.
Socialist government briefly in power.
American food aid staves off starvation.

1948 Right to strike limited.
General Tojo and six others hanged as war criminals.
Honda and Sony companies established.

1949 End of post-war 'baby boom'.
'Dodge Line' raises interest rates to end inflation.

1950 Outbreak of Korean war. 'Red purge' of Communists in trade unions.
National Police Reserve established.

1951 'Majority Peace' treaty signed.
US-Japan Security Treaty.

1952 Occupation ends.
'Reverse course' begins to reassert powers of central government over police and education.
Radio Japan established to broadcast Japanese news and current affairs commentary to neighbouring countries.

1953 End of Korean war.
Pre-war living standards restored.
TV broadcasting begins.

1954 Self-Decence Forces established.
Japanese fishermen catch radiation disease from US H-bomb tests in the Pacific.
Japan Air Lines begins trans-Pacific flights.

1955 'Five Year Plan for Economic Self-Support' published.
Japan Socialist Party factions re-united.
Liberal Democratic Party established.
Hiroshima Maidens visit US for surgery.

1956 Diplomatic relations re-established with USSR.
Local education boards to be appointed rather than elected.
Japan joins UN.

1957 First post-war defence policy statement.

1958 Japan launches world's largest oil-tanker to date.
Typhoon kills 1300.
Japan External Trade Organization established to promote exports.

1959 Crown Prince Akihito marries a commoner.

1960 Security Treaty crisis.
Ikeda announces 'income-doubling' plan.
Colour TV broadcasting begins.
US paroles last Japanese war criminals.
Assassination of Asanuma, leader of Japan Socialist Party.

1962 Japan and US settle Japanese contribution to costs of Occupation.

1964 Tokyo hosts Olympic Games.
Japan joins Organization for Economic Co-operation and Development (the 'club' of rich nations).

1965 Public Nuisance Prevention Corporation established.
Re-establishment of diplomatic relations with Republic of Korea.
Japan Overseas Co-Operation Volunteers established to send young volunteers to work in developing countries.

1966 Japan begins generating nuclear power.

1967 Japan's population exceeds 100,000,000.
Basic Environmental Pollution Law passed.

1968 Japan's balance of payments moves into surplus.
Student riots at Tokyo University.
Kawabata Yasunari wins Nobel Prize for Literature.

1969 Tomei Expressway establishes motorway link between Tokyo and Nagoya.

1970 Suicide of Mishima Yukio.
Japan produces its first industrial robot.
Expo '70 at Osaka.

1971 Environment Agency established.
Nixon shocks.
Three die in anti-airport protests at building of Narita.
Emperor Hirohito visits Europe.

1972 Tanaka's 'Plan to Remodel the Japanese Archipelago'.
Okinawa reverts to Japan.
Tanaka visits Mao Zedong.
Winter Olympics in Sapporo.

1973 Oil crisis.
Japanese Embassy opened in Beijing.

1974 Japan International Co-Operation Agency established to promote technical assistance for developing countries.
Ex Prime Minister Sato Eisaku receives Nobel Prize for Peace.

1975 State Visit of Queen Elizabeth II to Japan.

1976 Lockheed scandal.
MIG pilot lands at Hakodate, exposing weakness of air defence system.

1977 50 per cent of Japanese population born since 1945.

1978 Treaty of Peace and Friendship with People's Republic of China.
Resignatgion of General Kurisu.
Narita Airport opened.

1979 Second oil crisis.

Summit of seven leading industrial nations meets in Tokyo.

1980 Paul McCartney deported on drugs charge.

1981 Honda and British Leyland announce technical co-operation.

1982 Methane gas explosion kills 94 miners.

1983 Nagasaki Holland village opened as historical tourist attraction.

1984 Centre for International Co-Operation in Computerization established by 65 Japanese computer companies.

1985 Yen revalued by 40 per cent against US dollar.

517 killed near Tokyo in world's worst ever air crash involving a single aircraft.

1986 Nissan opens car factory in UK.
Prince Charles and Princess Diana visit Japan.
Maekawa report calls for opening of Japanese economy to foreign exports and participation.

1987 Japan pledges to double number of Japanese tourists by 1991.

1988 Japan becomes world's largest creditor nation and largest donor of foreign aid.
Prime Minister Takeshita pledges Japan to greater internationalization.

1989 Emperor Hirohito dies, ending the longest reign in Japanese history.

Prime Ministers of Japan

May 1946 Yoshida Shigeru
May 1947 Katayama Tetsu
Mar 1948 Ashida Hitoshi
Oct 1948 Yoshida Shigeru
Dec 1954 Hatoyama Ichiro
Dec 1956 Ishibashi Tanzan
Feb 1957 Kishi Nobusuke
Jul 1960 Ikeda Hayato
Nov 1964 Sato Eisaku
Jul 1972 Tanaka Kakuei
Dec 1974 Miki Takeo
Dec 1976 Fukuda Takeo
Dec 1978 Ohira Masayoshi
Jul 1980 Suzuki Zenko
Nov 1982 Nakasone Yasuhiro
Oct 1987 Takeshita Noburu

SKETCHES OF IMPORTANT FIGURES

Asanuma Inejiro (1898-1960) A politics graduate from Waseda University, Asanuma quickly became involved in the political struggles of radically-minded farmers in the 1920s. His wide political experience also included service as a Tokyo City Councillor and member of the Diet. In 1945 he helped to form the Japan Socialist Party, becoming its chief secretary in 1948. In 1960 he played a leading part in the protests against the revision of the US Security Treaty. Later that year he was assassinated at a public meeting by a right-wing fanatic. His simple lifestyle and modest personal manner won him many admirers.

Fukuda Takeo (1905-) A law graduate of Tokyo University, Fukuda became a high-flying official in the Ministry of Finance. Accused of corruption in 1948, he was eventually cleared in 1958. Switching to politics, he joined the Kishi faction of the LDP and eventually inherited it, serving as Finance Minister (1965-6, 1968-70 and 1973-4), Foreign Minister (1971-2) and Deputy Prime Minister (1974-6). An efficient administrator, he was unloved as Prime Minister (1976-8).

Hatoyama Ichiro (1883-1959) A lawyer and politician, born the son of a lawyer and politician, Hatoyama served 15 times as a member of the Lower House of the Diet. In 1945 he became the founding president of the revived Liberal Party but was purged from public life on the orders of SCAP. Readmitted to politics in 1951, he opposed Yoshida's leadership by establishing the Democratic Party in 1954, with himself as President. He became Prime Minister with the support of the Socialists but then switched direction to merge with his former rivals, creating the Liberal Democratic Party with himself as President. His most important achievement was the re-establishment of diplomatic links with the USSR in 1956, though he failed in his attempt to revise Article 9 of the Constitution.

Hiratsuka Raicho (1886-1971) Veteran leader of the women's movement, she founded the women's literary magazine *Seito* (*Bluestocking*) in 1911 and from 1920 campaigned for women's suffrage, education and consumers' interests. In the post-war period she was a strong supporter of the new constitution, which guaranteed women's political and legal equality with men. In 1953 she became President of the Feneration of Japanese Women's organizations and in 1954 launched a 'Japanese Women's Appeal', calling on the women of the world to help ban the H-bomb.

Emperor Hirohito (1901-89) Regent for the Emperor Taisho from 1921 onwards, Hirohito succeeded him on his death in 1926 and took the reign-name of 'Showa' to become the longest-reigning monarch in Japanese history. A constitutional ruler by personal preference, he nevertheless is believed to have exerted a decisive personal influence on three important occasions – to suppress the 26 February 1936 uprising, in which young officers attempted to seize power in his name; to bring the war to an end in August 1945; and publicly to renounce his 'divine' status in his New Year's Day message in January 1946. A distinguished marine biologist, the Emperor's personal tastes were simple and scholarly. In the post-war period he was seen much more in public, taking part in social and cultural occasions.

Ikeda Hayato (1899-1965) Having studied law at Kyoto University, he became an official of the Finance Ministry and successively Deputy Finance Minister (1947-8), Finance Minister (1949-52, 1956-7) and Minister of International Trade and Industry (1959-60). As Prime Minister (1960-4), he continued to make the economy his main priority, with an income-doubling plan which confirmed Japan's ambition to become an economic superpower.

Ishibashi Tanzan (1884-1973) The son of a Buddhist priest, Ishibashi studied literature at Waseda University and from 1911 to 1946 worked on the *Toyo Keizai Shimpo* (*Oriental Economic Journal*), becoming an expert on trade and industry. Serving briefly as Finance minister in Yoshida's first cabinet in 1946, he was banned from public life by SCAP from 1947 to 1951. In 1954 he helped Hatoyama establish the Democratic Party and served him as Minister of International Trade and Industry until succeeding him as Prime Minister. Illness led to his resignation after three months. Although a conservative, he devoted much effort to promoting closer links with China and the USSR.

Katayama Tetsu (1887-1978) The son of a lawyer father and Christian mother, Katayama became both and lent his services to the struggle for workers' and farmers' rights. In 1945 he played a key part in establishing the Japan Socialist Party and in 1948 served briefly as Japan's only socialist Prime Minister, until his coalition fell apart over his wage and price control policy. In 1953 he became president of the National League for the Protection of the Constitution. In 1960 he became senior adviser to the newly-established Democratic Socialist Party, a break-away group from the JSP. He was also renowned as an expert on classical Chinese poetry.

Kishi Nobusuke (1896-) Elder brother of Prime Minister Sato Eisaku, he studied law at Tokyo University, entered the civil service and played an energetic part in the industrial development of Manchuria (1936-40) and the organization of Japan's economy for war. Out of political life until 1952, he served Ishibashi as Minister of Foreign Affairs before succeeding him as Prime Minister in 1957. His main achievement was the controversial revision of the US Security Treaty in 1960. He resigned almost immediately afterwards but remained a strong anti-Communist and supported Japanese self-defence.

Miki Takeo (1907-88) US-educated Miki was elected to the Diet in 1937 as its youngest member and remained a member continuously thereafter, progressing via various minor parties to become secretary of the LDP in 1956. He served as Minister of International Trade and Industry (1965-6), Foreign Minister (1966-8) and Deputy Prime Minister (1972-4) before becoming Prime Minister (1974-6) as a compromise candidate to avoid a major split between the Ohira and Fukuda factions. His attempts to limit the influence of big business on politics foundered – on the strength of business-backed opposition – despite its popularity with the electors.

Mishima Yukio (1925-70) Japan's most famour post-war writer was educated at a school for aristocrats but rejected as unfit for military service during the War. He achieved early fame after the publication of his first novel *Confessions of a Mask* in 1948. A writer of great power and versatility, he combined a sophisticated understanding of Western culture with a passionate concern to preserve the integrity of Japanese tradition. Attracted to romantic nationalism, he became obsessed with body-building and the martial arts and established his own private army, the 'Shield Society', theoretically to aid the defence forces in the event of invasion or a Communist uprising. In 1970, having completed his major four-novel masterpiece *The Sea of Fertility*, he briefly seized control of the offices of a Tokyo SDF garrison commander. His speech to the curious troops, calling on them to return to traditional Japanese values, fell on deaf ears and he committed ritual suicide with the aid of devoted followers of the Shield Society.

Nakasone Yasuhiro (1918-) After serving as an officer in the Imperial Japanese navy in the closing stages of the war, he was elected to the lower house of the Diet in 1947 and has remained a member ever since. He served Sato as Minister of Transport and was also Director-General of the Defence Agency before holding office as Prime Minister (1982-7). His premiership was marked by his concern that Japan should play a more active and self-confident role in world affairs.

Nosaka Sanzo (1892-) Involved in the labour movement from his student days, Nosaka was a founding member of the British Communist Party (1920), before being deported. After visiting France, Germany and the USSR he returned to join the Japanese Communist Party and was arrested and imprisoned for his Communist activities in 1923 and 1928. From 1931 to 1946 he was in the USSR and China and made two undercover visits to America. In 1946 he was elected to the Diet but purged on MacArthur's orders in 1950. He returned to the Upper House of the Diet as party leader (1956-77) and served as chairman of the Central Committee of the party from 1958 to 1982.

Ohira Masayoshi (1910-80) Born the son of a farmer, Ohira worked in the finance Ministry before being elected to the Diet in 1952 and serving as Foreign Minister (1962-4), Minister of International Trade and Industry (1968-70) and Finance Minister (1974-6). In 1970 he took over leadership of Ikeda's former faction of the LDP. After repeated efforts and a long campaign to build support both within the party and among the general public, he finally became Prime Minister in 1978. A middle of the road man in his approach, he was held in affection by many and won the nickname 'Papa' (Otochan). His sudden death during the 1980 election campaign may have contributed to the LDP's landslide victory by reuniting the party and winning it a sympathy vote.

Sato Eisaku (1901-75) Brother of Kishi Nobusuke, Sato studied law at Tokyo University and served in the Civil Service before switching to politics in 1948. He held the posts of Minister of Postal Services (1951-2), Construction (1952-3), Finance (1958-60) and International Trade and Industry (1961-2). Suspected of corruption over shipbuilding contracts, he was never actually arrested. His premiership (1964-72) was the longest in post-war Japanese history but he failed to pass the position on to his preferred successor, Fukuda Takeo. In 1974 he was awarded the Nobel Prize for Peace for his consistent opposition to nuclear weapons.

Tanaka Kakuei (1918-) A self-made man, he entered the Diet in 1947 and served as Minister of Postal Services, Minister of Finance and Minister of International Trade and Industry, and Secretary-General of the LDP before becoming Prime Minister (1972-4), the first non university graduate to achieve this office since World War I. Deposed after allegations of corruption, and arrested in 1976 in connection with the Lockheed scandal, he was eventually found guilty and sentenced but remained at liberty by lodging a series of appeals. He continued to play an important political role behind the scenes.

Yoshida, Shigeru (1878-1967) Born the son of a Liberal Party leader, Yoshida studied politics at Tokyo University and, entering the diplomatic service, rose swiftly to become Japanese Ambassador to Italy and Great Britain. His pro-western views kept him out of office during the war years and when he tried to join in attempts to arrange a negotiated peace he was arrested by the military police. As leader of the Liberal Party from 1946 onwards, he formed five cabinets before his high-handed style led to a loss of support which forced him to resign in 1954. Chief architect of the controversial 'majority peace', enshrined in the 1951 San Francisco Peace Treaty, he was a firm advocate of the American alliance and a supporter of limited rearmament. Noted for his personal charm and humour, he was honoured with a state funeral on his death.

BOOK LIST

General

W.G. Beasley, *The Modern History of Japan*, Weidenfeld & Nicolson 3rd ed. 1981

Roger Buckley, *Japan Today*, Cambridge UP 1985

G. Richard Storry, *A History of Modern Japan*, Penguin 1968

Dick Wilson, *The Sun at Noon: An Anatomy of Modern Japan*, Coronet 1988

Particular Aspects

D.E. Apter and Nagayo Sawa, *Against the State: Politics and Social Protest in Japan*, Harvard UP 1984. A study of the opposition to the building of Narita International airport

Hans H. Baerwald, *Party Politics in Japan*, Allen & Unwin 1986

Rodney Barker, *The Hiroshima Maidens*, Penguin 1986. Aftermath of nuclear war – an account of the impact on America of disfigured girls seeking plastic surgery

G. Daniel and R. Drifte (eds), *Europe and Japan: Changing Relationships since 1945*, Paul Norbury 1986

Joy Hendry, *Understanding Japanese Society*, Croom-Helm 1987

John Hersey, *Hiroshima*, Penguin 1946. Classic account, many times reprinted, based on eyewitness reactions

Malcolm McIntosh, *Japan Re-Armed*, Frances Pinter 1986

Satoshi Komata, *Japan in the Passing Lane*, Unwin 1982. Insider account of life in a Japanese car factory

Richard Tames, *Passport to Japan*, Franklin Watts 1988. Colour illustrated account of contemporary lifestyles

INDEX

The Japanese put their surname, or family name, first. This index, and the preceding *Sketches of Important Figures*, follows this practice.